ALL YOUR FRIENDS LIKE THIS

HAL CRAWFORD, ANDREW HUNTER & DOMAGOJ FILIPOVIC

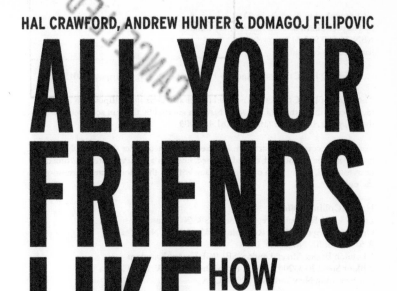

ALL YOUR FRIENDS LIKE THIS

HOW SOCIAL NETWORKS TOOK OVER NEWS

HarperCollins*Publishers*

HarperCollins*Publishers*

First published in Australia in 2015
by HarperCollins*Publishers* Australia Pty Limited
ABN 36 009 913 517
harpercollins.com.au

HarperCollins*Publishers*
Level 13, 201 Elizabeth Street, Sydney NSW 2000, Australia
Unit D1, 63 Apollo Drive, Rosedale, Auckland 0632, New Zealand
A 53, Sector 57, Noida, UP, India
1 London Bridge Street, London, SE1 9GF, United Kingdom
2 Bloor Street East, 20th floor, Toronto, Ontario M4W 1A8, Canada
195 Broadway, New York NY 10007, USA

National Library of Australia Cataloguing-in-Publication entry

Crawford, Hal, author.
  All your friends like this : how social networks took over
  news / Hal Crawford, Andrew Hunter,
  Domagoj Filipovic.
  ISBN: 978 1 4607 5068 1 (paperback)
  ISBN: 978 1 4607 0526 1 (ebook)
  Online social networks – Social aspects.
  Digital media – Social aspects.
  Broadcast journalism – Forecasting.
  Mass media – Audiences.
  Mass media – Social aspects
  Other Creators/Contributors:
  Hunter, Andrew, author.
  Filipovic, Domagoj, author.
302.30285

Cover design by Hazel Lam, HarperCollins Design Studio
Cover images by retales botijero / Getty Images
Infographics by Sam Williams
Internal images page 37 by shutterstock.com, and ninemsn;
page 278 courtesy Christine Von Pein
Typeset in Adobe Caslon Pro by Kirby Jones
Printed and bound in Australia by Griffin Press
The papers used by HarperCollins in the manufacture of this book are a natural,
recyclable product made from wood grown in sustainable plantation forests.
The fibre source and manufacturing processes meet recognised international
environmental standards, and carry certification.

Contents

Contents

Acknowledgements

23 people who ~~helped with this book~~ restored our faith in humanity:

Rachel Hynes (for love, guidance and killer copy editing)

Tina Filipovic (for the love, support and proof reading)

Iris Huizinga (for patience and unswerving belief)

Shaun Davies (the 'fourth member' of Share Wars, for shaping early thinking)

Brigid Delaney (for help in navigating the literary world)

Tim Dunlop (for truly believing)

Paul Colgan (for media insights)

Sean Maher (for mostly constructive criticism)

Jenny Duxbury (for the fervour)

Natalie Sutton (for spreading the Like)

Antonia Christie (for opening doors)

Fiona Inglis (for awesome representation and understanding)

Mary Rennie (for fearless editing prowess)

Catherine Milne (for knowing how to handle fragile egos)

Benjamin Stevenson (for stress-testing the material)

Emma Dowden (for the proofing and the pain we had to have)

Rory Kinsella (for the wisdom at the marble tables)

Emma Chamberlain (for making it real)

Henri Paget (for the Oracle, among many creations)

Marko Filipovic (for being wiser than you act)

Marica Filipovic (for proof reading and advice)

Matthew Janis (for testing our logic)

Andrew Banks (for a story)

Prologue

There is a wonderful scene in Annie Dillard's rambling book *Pilgrim at Tinker Creek* where she comes across a frog on the edge of the water one day. Dillard explains she has been getting better and better at spotting frogs, and delights in scaring them into the creek. This frog doesn't budge. It's a small frog, with 'wide, dull eyes'. She manages to get within a few feet of it when she realises something else is at play. Something dark and weird. The frog begins to collapse.

> The spirit vanished from his eyes as if snuffed. His skin emptied and drooped; his very skull seemed to collapse and settle like a kicked tent. He was shrinking before my eyes like a deflating football.

The frog had fallen prey to a giant water bug. This carnivorous insect dissolves its victims from the inside by injecting them with saliva, then sucking out the goop. The bug had been there, under the waterline, the whole time Dillard was sneaking up on the frog – drinking the life out of it.

Most observers of news media share Dillard's perspective. Digital platforms have been drinking the life out of traditional publishers from below the waterline, while the façade of their prey has remained more or less intact. Newspapers, radio and television stations still publish and broadcast to millions but the numbers are clear: in an era when advertising money is moving to digital, more than 50 cents of every digital dollar goes to Facebook and Google. Far from colonising digital, traditional media's share of the digital spend has in most cases stalled.

Those numbers have obscured the good that has come out of the shift in media power. All anyone cares about is how that poor frog is going to get on without any insides. That's because the old media have more or less owned the discussion – it's been the guy with the 'wide, dull eyes' talking. It's time to get below the surface and find out what is happening.

What you find below the waterline is a strange world where the predator–prey relationship is gone and weird forms of symbiosis emerge. Digital platforms dole out some of their massive bounty to content creators in order to ensure their own continued prosperity. Bedrock values like telling the truth are challenged. What people really value is laid bare.

What we do in this book is sketch one of the aspects of this strange world: the impact that social networks have on the type of news we consume. We invite you to come in. The water is lovely, despite the whiff of swamp.

A note on the structure of the book: each chapter has been written by one us – Hal, Andy or Dom. We veer between the personal and the objective, but always we have tried to 'walk our talk' by using examples. If you find yourself wondering why you are reading about starlets, monks or kids' entertainment at any point, be assured there is method to the madness. The stories form the background and texture against which we have made our observations, and we can guarantee you'll be engaged. The social network has seen to that. These are the world's most likeable stories.

Chapter 1

Why Sharing is Important

By Hal Crawford

There are two reasons you should care about social networks if you care about news.

First, sharing on social networks has become a major distribution mechanism for news stories. The digitisation of social networks has augmented a natural process – and for millions of people their first exposure to information about the world comes from their friends, not directly from news media.

The second reason hinges on the first. Like all distribution mechanisms, social networks influence the content they distribute. It turns out that people on social networks prefer certain styles and types of content. The stories change and with them the tone and flavour of the newsmaking process are altered.

Social networks are one of the main drivers in a process that has seen the guts sucked out of traditional news outfits and sprayed all over the joint, allowing new players to spring up and different types of storytelling to flourish. They have made news better while opening the door to unprecedented abuses. That's why this book matters, and why we have done everything we can to find out what makes news stories share on social networks.

The good old days

Paul Murray edited *The West Australian* newspaper for the whole of the 1990s – a neat decade. Halfway through his tenure I started at the paper as a cadet reporter.

The West began in 1833 as a colonial gazette. Tabloid in physical size, the mainstream paper of record for the city of Perth had managed to outlast or outcompete all its rivals, so that by the 1990s we were the only show in town. Everyone said we had distribution stitched up – the newsagencies, the subscriptions, and the army of trucks and planes needed to get that paper to the whole state. Western Australia is massive – three-and-a-half times the size of Texas – and we had early deadlines for the state editions to get out and onto planes heading north. You filed a story at 7pm and someone would be reading it at 6am the next day 2200 kilometres away in Kununurra. The effort involved in printing and shifting those physical papers was immense, almost heroic, and now it all seems like the labour of ants.

The West had a culture that I now know is common to newspapers across the world. I started fresh from university, so I had to be reprogrammed: I had to stop writing to make myself look smart and start communicating. There is something wonderful in newspaper culture, for those not acquainted with it; something valuable in the wisdom created by innumerable interactions with society at every level. Everything was honed for clear communication and fast production: the concept of a style guide, arbitrary but inviolable; the way subeditors tore your copy up and stitched it back together; and above all, the knowledge of what made a good story. After years of trying to guess what university professors wanted to hear, I lapped it up: certainty and reality. Progress at the paper centred on the story, and in the craft of its creation there was a well-founded clarity. 'Nice yarn' was the highest praise possible.

All this rested on a typical newspaper hierarchy. At the bottom were the cadets, then the reporters and subeditors, the senior reporters or roundsmen, the chief of staff, the back bench editors, section editors and, above them all, the editor. Position in the hierarchy corresponded to who knew stories best – the editor was the ultimate judge of story.

Paul Murray was a big man. He was called 'Mooner'. The cadet supervisor told us this was because when he was younger he had 'moonlighted' as a journalist a lot. None of us believed that, and no plausible answer ever surfaced, but neither his size nor the indignity of his nickname mattered. Mooner was like an old-school god to us – distant, terrifying and deserving of respect. We were told of his battles with the government, of his fastidious work in reporting and how in his day he had earned front page after front page with his stories. In the newspaper world this is where the cultural rubber hits the road: the mythologising of the struggle against authority, the cult of the truth-teller, the byline counts. The most important 'yarn' of all is the story of the stories.

After a few months of cultural indoctrination as a cadet I was invited to the afternoon news conference. All I knew about it was that it was the meeting where the editors decided what would be in the paper the next day.

The West was at that time working out of a building called Westralia Square on St Georges Terrace in the centre of Perth. Old-timers would affectionately talk about the days when they had occupied Newspaper House down the road; in that venerable place you could literally feel the paper being made as the basement presses started up every evening. It's a common motif in the media industry that sits well with the rest of the mythology: authenticity resides in the past, the present is wretched and the future diabolical.

Westralia Square was a bland place. Out the front was Rigby's, a bar that managed to institutionalise the media's problematic consumption of alcohol without any style whatsoever. Inside the newsroom was a modular interior that would have done for any accountancy or law firm anywhere in the world. The afternoon news conference was held in one of the glass-sided offices that looked out over the Perth CBD; there lay one of the most isolated cities in the world, reproducing in miniature the structures and functions of western culture.

Around the room stood the editors: an odd bunch of men and women. Rumour had it that one of them had inadvertently sent Mooner an electronic note referring to him as 'the fat cunt in the corner' and had subsequently not spoken to his editor-in-chief for the past year. A roomful of characters. The night editor was perpetually tired and struggled to be nice; the features editor was jolly and round; the business editor a smooth prodigy; the jowly senior police reporter would later teach me to operate in the field. There were more than 10 people present. They all waited around a table covered in photographs, placed face-down. Then Mooner entered.

I had braced myself for a bunfight but it was a surprisingly sombre affair. The editors offered their stories, the room considered them as one would consider a fine wine, and then Mooner passed judgement. He was not particularly brutal; he didn't have to be. He spoke with authority and consideration. Occasionally he growled that something was 'shit'. It seemed to me, the cadet in the corner, that there was menace underlying his performance. He could 'tear you a new one'. But it was all, even the threat of attack, backed up by expertise. What was important, what was entertaining, what was a nice yarn.

The main pages and story positions were dealt with, leaving someone else the job of choosing the filler stories. The final part of the conference was considering what picture would lead the front page. The chief photographer revealed his photographs one by one, flipping over the A4 prints on the table for the consideration of the room. He liked a picture of a submarine. Others liked the footballers. Then he turned over a picture of a pig and child playing together.

'That's the one,' said Mooner.

He was right. The picture of the pig and the child playing together was the best. It popped out. Everyone was satisfied, even the photographer, and I didn't ask myself how Mooner knew which one was the best. It seemed obvious. It was my story, and I had just bought into the system big time.

Reign of the alpha male

What I now perceive, coming from a digital perspective, is that editors like Paul Murray were working in an information vacuum. The audience and what they liked to consume may have been the basis for the 'nice yarn' in theory, but there was no way in practice the editor had a sufficiently granular level of feedback to know whether his selection was justified.

Think about what was available to newspaper editors in terms of actual hard data about story selection. The only real evidence was circulation figures. In the 1990s these came out daily, for the previous day, and included newsagency sales, subscriptions and giveaways all rolled into one. Attributing variations in sales to any single story was an exercise in blind faith unless the story was so big, like the death of Diana, that copies actually ran out. But one problem with the biggest stories is that generally all your competitors have the same material; it's what they do on the quiet days that sets news publishers apart. The other issue is that big stories generally tell you nothing you don't already know. Experienced newspaper editors say they have always been hungry for real information about their audience, but distrust both circulation figures and the market research conducted by their own advertising departments.

Aside from circulation, there was only the folk wisdom of the newsroom to work out what constituted a good story. This was based on a journalist's own feelings about what was interesting. There was a lot of craft and creativity but very little science in newsroom culture. The editor's statements on the quality of stories were unverifiable – they were only subject to dispute by others equally ignorant as to their success or failure with the audience. In a situation like that, whose voice is going to triumph?

The alpha male's, of course.

One of the great Australian newspaper editors in the 'tear them a new one' mould is Col Allan. A News Corporation man, Allan edited Sydney's *Daily Telegraph* in the 1990s and was exported to run the *New York Post* in the new century.

According to colleagues, Allan is 'insanely aggressive' and widely regarded as 'a terrifying force' at News. One editor who worked with Allan for years describes him as 'a man who never had to learn manners'.

'He's the kind of guy who if you're in a meeting with him, you won't get a word in edgewise,' says the editor. 'He's got the R.M. Williams boots up on the table – he's a man who's very comfortable with his own power.'

Allan was famous in his Australian days for urinating into a washbasin in his office while in meetings, behaviour verified by editiors in the room at the time.

Former journalist Paul Sheridan corroborates the fear that Allan generated in rank-and-file reporters.

I was at *The Tele* prior to the Holt Street refit, and the newsroom was basically just one vast room. You could still see the line where the wall between where the old

Telegraph and the old *Sun* had been. In the centre of the newsroom was the kitchen. The kitchen was very Spartan. There were a couple of old, dilapidated cupboards. There was a perpetually boiling urn. There was the caterers' pack of International Roast. And there was a teaspoon, attached to a chain. The chain was connected to the cupboard, and the teaspoon had been there so long half of it had worn away. Half of the spoon was gone.

I remember walking into the kitchen one day and there's Col, making himself a cup of coffee. I had no idea that the guy even knew who I was. It was very early on in my time at *The Tele*. I had written a story – it was summer, and there'd been violent storms. I'd written the story and this was the day after it had been published. Col just looked at me. He goes:

'Mate, is "forecasted" a fucking word?'

'Urm . . . no.'

'Well don't put it in my fucking copy again. If I could throw this fucking spoon at you, I would.'

I'm surprised I didn't wet myself on the spot. That's the type of guy he was. He knew everything that was happening around him. It was his domain.

Sheridan says he never heard praise from Allan.

You'd get this phone call and you'd pick up the phone – you didn't know it was Col calling you – and he'd go:

'What was the last thing on the wires?'

'Um . . . the weather?'

'No, shithead.'

It was a little game he played. I was terrified of him. I thought I was going to lose my job because I didn't know the last slugline.

My observation of Col was that, yes, he was a hangover from the hard era of journalism – and there were casualties of that era - but equally it was exciting. It was exciting to be part of a hard newspaper culture that said 'fuck you' to the establishment. You felt the power.

Allan's power in those glory days was primal – whether while browbeating his people, urinating in conference, or picking his headlines. It is no accident that the notorious alpha male editor should also be an enemy of using data to make decisions.

When Allan was visiting Sydney in 2013 to review Australian newspaper operations, he delivered a speech to editors that opposed the blind use of data and proposed that editors needed to go back to using their instinct.

The speech was seen within News Corp as an attack on then chief executive Kim Williams, who had attempted to force a data-based approach on Australian editors. At the start of his short tenure, Williams urged journalists to stop using their 'tummy compasses' and start looking at the hard evidence of what readers were doing. It was his attempt to change a media culture that was having trouble adapting to the digital world.

It's difficult to get a direct quote from Allan's speech – the meeting is a kind of sacred pow-wow for senior News editorial staff and sources say they doubt anyone recorded it – but *The Australian* newspaper later described it as 'empowering' and a rally cry that had 'fired everyone up'.

Allan's position is a good illustration of where media finds itself today. In this scenario he represents not corporate management but newspaper culture all the way from cadet to editor, the heart of the newsroom production style that was born in an era when almost nothing was known about the audience. In this old media world, gut instinct was relied on by necessity. Strong leaders work in uncertain times and any direction is better than none in an information vacuum.

The history of newspapers in the 20th century is full of anti-hero leaders in the Allan mould: potty-mouthed oddballs who enjoy sticking it up the establishment while making millions of dollars for the owners of their publications. Fierce individualists who speak to millions. Misanthropes with hearts of gold who snap out decisions and are addicted to news. They tend not to become household names – the fame of editors is restricted – but within the industry this has been the model of leadership. It's a style that allowed newspapers to keep audiences engaged, maintain a measure of independence and inspire intelligent people to keep working for them.

But what worked once is no longer valid. The addiction to the 'tummy compass' is one of the bindweeds of old media. The cult of the alpha male editor with its attendant blindness to data now represents a dark side that will work against any organisation still subscribing to it. This is not controversial in digital media. The reality is that the kind of problem represented by Col Allan was settled a long time ago, at the beginning of the digital news era in the early 2000s. It was settled as soon as online editors began seeing what audiences actually clicked on.

The Spears spike

By 2007 Britney Spears had blossomed: she had moved on from mere pop stardom and had become a focal point for an industry. The girl from Kentwood, Louisiana, who got her break in the Mickey Mouse Club had worked hard at being the centre of attention and now, as the stress cracks began to show, she had her wish on the grandest scale possible. A global online news audience in the millions watched as Britney melted down in discrete and regular doses.

The stage had been set in 2006 with Spears divorcing Kevin Federline, being investigated by child protection agencies, almost dropping her baby boy on camera, partying with Lindsay Lohan and Paris Hilton, and publicly adopting a no-underpants policy. These wild times coincided with the coming of age of gossip sites like PerezHilton.com and TMZ, and the mainstream consumption of gossip on general news sites.

The result was that as 2007 began, Spears was followed constantly by a pack of photographers and journalists. According to one member of this motley crew, the gig was surreal. Most nights a convoy of 30 cars crisscrossed Los Angeles as a mentally unstable Spears alternately courted and fled the mob. As noted in Steve Dennis's biography *Britney: Inside the Dream*, road rules were thrown out the window. 'It didn't matter what else was happening on the road. When she turned, we turned, all 30 of us … it's a scary type of mayhem.'

The paps were the physical manifestation of the new media, and Spears's weirdly symbiotic relationship with the pack spoke to wider co-dependency. They represented an audience bigger and more fickle – more willing to move on to the next thing – than any the world had seen before. Spears obediently fed this beast, shaving her head one night in a salon in Tarzana, California, then attacking a pap with an umbrella, then putting in a memorably zombie-like performance at the MTV Video Music Awards. She was working the medium.

The vapidity of the subject matter – and the fact that, contrary to expectations, Spears didn't die – have ensured a kind of amnesia around the immense popularity and traffic-generating power of the former Mouseketeer back then. Databases don't forget, however, and the traffic records of the biggest Australian portal, ninemsn, show that in 2007 Spears alone was generating more than a million page views every month.

The important point about Spears's traffic-generating ability, and the difference from past pop sensations, is that editors knew about it in real time. This is the gulf between old and new media. The Spears spike was so intense because of a feedback loop created by new digital tools that showed editors who was reading what in tiny increments. This loop happens when editors see what is being read, and very quickly give more of the same to the audience while culling underperforming stories. At BuzzFeed, a social news site that started in 2006, this strategy of culling stories is called 'starving the losers'. The positive part of the loop, what you might call 'feeding the winners', results in runaway spikes of news activity on popular subjects.

The analytical tools that allow this to happen were primitive back then, but they changed the game nonetheless. Software such as Omniture and Google Analytics allowed editors to see not just overall audience size to a site, but also which content was being clicked on and how long users stayed there. In those days, Omniture updated its data every five minutes. Compare the difference: a daily newspaper editor publishes in 24-hour increments, and receives sketchy data on gross performance of the whole publication another 24 hours after that. An online editor publishes several hundred times a day and receives performance data down to article level in real time. Everything changes in this new world because at last it is possible to respond to audience preference quickly. Starving the losers won't win you a Pulitzer but in a world where page views equal money it pays the bills.

The adoption of the practice of real-time traffic monitoring and response didn't happen overnight. Tools like Omniture had been around, sampling traffic in very small increments, for years before editors changed the mindsets they had inherited from offline media. The makers of the analytical software themselves didn't even realise they had created real-time editorial tools – Omniture was supposed to be reporting software, the kind of thing a business manager would use at the end of the week or month. To make it operate in real time at ninemsn (where I was working by then) it was overlaid with a manual process called 'The Oracle' that compared actual article performance with expectations. It would be 2013 before Adobe, Omniture's owners, added explicit interface layers to make monitoring performance in real time easy.

So it took time and pressure before editors shifted their thinking. When they did, they discovered a new way of knowing their audience – an audience that, it turned out, did not conform to old media ideas of what was important. Apparently people really wanted to read about people like Lohan, Hilton and Spears. It was shocking.

For me the symbolic high-water mark of this discovery of the audience and how to capture serious traffic was 14 January 2008. More than a year after Spears began her meltdown came a climax of sorts, a child custody hearing at the LA Superior Court. Hundreds of reporters with attendant TV crews and gear had converged. Paps were standing on roofs to get a better angle while choppers hovered overhead, and there was a lot of jostling and rivalry. As an MSNBC reporter commented in a live cross, 'It's a zoo. Is this not embarrassing?' Yes, and the audience loved it.

Into this shameful congregation drove a black Cadillac SUV. Out of the Cadillac emerged Sam Lutfi, Adnan Ghalib and Britney Spears. An interesting trio. Lutfi, a nonentity who had wormed his way into Spears's inner circle, was standing in as her manager and media advisor although he had no media experience. Ghalib was a paparazzo who had been following Spears for a year before he crossed the line and started going out with her. Now the three of them, their backs to the Cadillac, faced the massive media scrum. Spears, wearing a wig after her self-inflicted shearing, was there to get her children back. She was no doubt medicated up to the eyeballs – accounts from the time say the singer was taking anti-anxiety and anti-psychotic drugs as well as prescribed uppers and downers – and as she became surrounded, the throng proved too much. She freaked out and headed back into the car. Her two knights joined her, the Cadillac took off and the chase began.

At ninemsn, on the other side of the world, we received chopper footage of this zany pursuit live. The stream was coming in on one of the dedicated international lines, and we took that footage and streamed it live on the site, updating the related article on the go. The audience loved it. Spears was still hot. Lutfi and Ghalib were opportunistic cads. The three of them were zigzagging, apparently aimlessly, in a madcap drive across LA. Back at court, Kevin Federline had shown up and actually made it into the building, and was being awarded continued custody of the children.

Meanwhile Lutfi, Ghalib and Spears stopped and got out of the car. They went into a small church. We were speculating in real time. Would Ghalib and Spears get married? Maybe this was the game they were playing, the three of them, visiting the Little Brown Church where Ronald and Nancy Reagan had been married in the 1950s. Paps piled into the church after them. Spears took a pen and started writing a note to God.

Freeze the frame. That's the exact high point, or the low point if you want to look at it that way. From that moment, despite Ghalib's best attempts and even a hospital sojourn for Spears, the shine started to wear off. Spears would check in to rehab, Ghalib would start peddling revealing video footage of the singer, and it all got dull and tawdry. More importantly for editors, the bottom fell out of the Spears traffic market: a year on at ninemsn, she had dipped from averaging a million page views a month to a mere 70,000. Another year after that and she was no more than a statistical error, food for web crawlers and sad wire agencies too far removed from the audience to smell digital death.

Trash is not who we are

Spears was a traffic spike and that spike subsided as expected. Other celebrities took Spears's place and continued to generate millions of page views. Sites like TMZ and PerezHilton.com kept serving stories to millions of people. They do so to this day. But the fire has gone out, and the craft of enticing an audience to click on a link is no longer the height of digital audience generation.

The change relates to something fascinating about the gossip news audience that you only discover when you go looking for it in the real world. It doesn't exist.

Digital editors make this discovery – at odds with every analytical tool at their disposal – every time they engage in qualitative audience research. When you ask people directly what type of news they like, the results are clear: very few want more celebrity news, while lovers of world news are thick on the ground. Get 10 people in a room and it's rare to find even one who prefers entertainment news to international affairs.

It's not dishonesty. It's just that almost no one identifies themselves as a 'Britney Spears' reader. While they may happen to click on a link and read a story, it doesn't define them as a person. 'Trash' is not who they are.

The reason I know it's not dishonesty is that I too am not a 'Britney Spears' reader. I just happen to have read a lot of articles about Spears. Sitting behind the two-way mirrors in user-testing bunkers, I learned that other people are just like me. All these teachers, tradesmen, sales reps, students and so on have very diverse interests – on which it is difficult to build a mainstream media business – but publicly they are united in their desire for better news on important subjects. Privately they all tend to be enticed by the same kind of articles. Very few people can resist clicking on a picture of Spears attacking a pap with an umbrella. After all, it says nothing about you and it costs you nothing. Why not take a look? It is vital as a publisher to remember that public statements give insight into aspirations rather than predict private behaviour.

This is the point: in a world of private information consumption, Spears is huge. Where news consumption is an individual act, isolated from social context, news editors really don't need to know anything more than what their analytical tools tell them. The moment consuming news becomes public the rules change and Spears bombs. It's like some kind of weird quantum state, where an observer can change reality. Just don't look inside the box and you can have your traffic.

In 2008 Facebook hit 100 million active users. The social network that began in 2004 as a 'hotness' rating tool for

Harvard undergraduates had busted out of its Ivy League ghetto and gone global. Facebook gave the internet a human face and brought things down to a friendly scale. The fact the network had millions of users was mostly irrelevant to those users, who built up a circle of people they knew. The internet suddenly became real: friends, colleagues, family members, all posting and chatting about everyday things. As in real-life interaction, people on Facebook relayed news and talked about events, and that had big implications for news publishers. On digital social networks, you don't have to say, 'Did you hear about X?' and then retell a story. You can just post a link to the article and it gets transmitted to your friends' feeds. You have achieved the socially necessary task of being a source of interesting information without the cognitive load of having to remember details.

From a publisher's point of view, audiences start arriving at articles directly from social networks, generating traffic in much the same way they would if they arrived from a home page. This is as true for Twitter and other social tools as it is for Facebook, but because of its scale Facebook was the first truly significant traffic generator for mainstream publishers. At the start of 2009 Facebook launched its 'Like' button – a widget that allowed publishers to incorporate the social network into their own sites directly – and the traffic flow began in earnest.

People on social networks become something like editors and publishers themselves in this new world, selecting stories they like and passing them on to their friends, who then consume the stories on the original publisher's website. The big difference here is that the public gaze has been injected into the process: you only publicise stories that work for you, socially. You consciously value them, or you judge that your social circle will value them, or you see some good to yourself or others arising as a result of their transmission. As the proportion of people arriving at news sites from social networks grows, so the types of stories that work on social networks get more exposure, and the news mix as a whole changes. Editors armed with sophisticated analytical tools that show them the provenance of their audiences then encourage a feedback loop by commissioning and promoting the types of stories they know work on social networks.

So what stories work on social networks?

'The part of us that loves animals is the best part of us,' says Jack Shepherd. 'Animals can also be a really good way of talking about humans.'

Shepherd is BuzzFeed's editorial director. His other title at the New York-based social news publisher is 'Beastmaster', an intentionally dorky reference to pop culture.

'It's an '80s movie. I don't know if you know it. A lot of people think it's horrible, but I always thought it was cool.'

Shepherd is blue-eyed, bearded, in his early thirties. He speaks with calm assurance and couldn't be more different from the model of an alpha male editor. Like the stories he publishes, he is immediately likeable.

BuzzFeed has been working on the question of what stories work on social networks since 2006, when very few other people cared.

'We were built to focus on what people share,' says Shepherd. '[But] we think of ourselves as a news organisation.'

The site was started as an experiment by Jonah Peretti, the man who co-founded *The Huffington Post*. Peretti wanted to find out if he could track and predict the stories that would go viral on social networks. At BuzzFeed's inception it was more machine-based aggregator than news publisher, but as it grew it employed journalists and editors, until it resembled something like a traditional media company in scope, if not culture. Like the site itself, Shepherd, who joined in 2008, has come at the news game backwards according to traditional media practice. He started at animal rights group PETA, thinking up stunts to get attention on social networks – one of his early hits was a campaign to rename fish 'sea kittens' in a bid to make them cuter to mainstream audiences.

'What people don't realise about [creating something popular on social networks] is that it takes a lot of time and craft,' Shepherd says. 'What seems light is actually the product of a lot of work.'

In the beginning Shepherd stayed with animals. Since the days of Aesop – and presumably before – animals have been one of the most powerful metaphorical tools in a storyteller's kit. Their power on social media is immense, and as we will see in Chapter 5, animals are one of the most commonly shared subjects. It seems appropriate that the Beastmaster rose within BuzzFeed to be the editor controlling all viral content creation.

Shepherd recognises the power of certain subjects but disavows a formulaic approach: 'Empathy is a big part of it

– having the ability to put yourself in another person's shoes. Put yourself in the shoes of the reader, or get a sense of what people will respond to based on your own visceral reaction. Get in that mindset and get good at it.'

A lot of people attack BuzzFeed's content mix – heavy on animals, lists, gay rights, nostalgia and politics – but Shepherd says the 'understandable but misguided' criticisms are coming from a confused and threatened industry.

'This is a new kind of news media – it's unique,' he says.

One of Shepherd's biggest insights is his explanation of how news audiences have had their expectations altered.

'People are now very used to getting information from their Facebook feed or their Twitter feed, and that mode of getting information is going to be lots of different things. You are going to see a cute picture of your nephew that your brother posted, you're going to see a cute cat picture, and then someone is going to post their wedding announcement, and then someone is going to post their link to serious news like election results. It's a very natural way for people to get news – it's just a different kind of news.'

That redefinition of news, so profoundly unsettling for old-school journalists, is reflected in an editorial culture that throws all sorts of traditions on the analytical bonfire. There are no 'pitch meetings' or conferences in Shepherd's Buzz Unit, only daily workshops at which writers talk about their story ideas. Shepherd says he doesn't slap bad ideas down – he doesn't need to, because the audience takes care of that.

'I'm always pleased if I think something won't work and then it does,' he says. 'You've learned something new.'

The incredible thing is that he believes it. I really can't see the Beastmaster tearing anyone a new anything. Compare this gentle man, pointing out that 'I don't think that story will really work, but go ahead anyway' with Col Allan standing at his basin issuing orders while pissing. The worlds are colliding right there, between the empathy and urine.

Shepherd's own favourite work is his '21 pictures that will restore your faith in humanity', a piece of content that pretty much does what it says on the tin. It has been shared 24,000 times on social networks and viewed more than 14 million times. That's a whole lot of faith restored.

There's a hard edge to the story, though – one that's not hinted at in the pictures of self-sacrifice and the captions celebrating generosity. At the top of the page is a red-on-grey bar that details total views (14,641,550 at time of writing) and something called 'social lift' (13x). Social lift is a measure of the proportion of the article traffic that came from social networks, as opposed to 'seed traffic' from the BuzzFeed network, and it's important to the organisation.

'If you get a spot on the home page and you don't get good social lift, you're in trouble. It's a wasted opportunity – we had that home-page traffic already, right? If something is worthy of a spot, it should be valued, it should work on social.'

It's the only time I've seen Shepherd frown. If the new editorial culture has a fuzzy exterior, this is the cold, hard centre. You are unconditionally accountable to the metrics and you can't get out of it with swagger, bluff and a shouty temper.

Chapter 2

The Birth of Share Wars

By Hal Crawford

Picture yourself on the verge of a job interview.

It's well known that assessment in a spoken interview has no correlation to subsequent success in the job. A general discussion designed to determine the character and 'cultural fit' of a candidate is a festival of delusion and cognitive bias. Daniel Kahneman, the Israeli-American Nobel Prize-winning psychologist whose work comes up several times in this book, established the principle while working for the Israeli Defence Forces, observing that expert interviews do little better than chance in predicting the future success of candidates. Interviewers are swayed by what people look like; how recently they spoke to them; their mood; and above all by the misplaced belief in their own prowess. It is unusual to come across anyone who rates themselves a bad judge of character. Interviews that rely on the intuition and expertise of the interviewer are almost useless.

The problem is that the charade suits both sides: neither the interviewers nor the interviewee care to admit they may as well be rolling dice. So job interviews persist, and everyone reading this book will have experienced the feeling of waiting outside the closed door while the panel sits within.

This is not about how well you can do the job. This is about how well you can be judged.

In July 2006 I was preparing for that judgement.

I'd left *The West Australian* newspaper eight years before and gone wandering the world, returning to Australia to work at La Trobe University in Melbourne. I was teaching a journalism course – an education I had never believed in. My problem, as I saw these hundreds of sleepy faces assembled for the morning lecture, was that journalism didn't seem to me to be a fit object of study. The practice itself is a combination of mundane technicalities (details better learned on the job), general knowledge and curiosity. How do you teach it, really? Maybe my scepticism seeped out. The university decided not to renew my contract for the next semester, which left me with two weeks to find a new source of income. My girlfriend and I had enough money left for Plan B – two tickets back to Perth.

I was becoming desperate. I had applied for jobs I thought I could do pretty well. Little reporting gigs, like writing shipping news for *Lloyd's List*. Stuff in public relations (how hard could it be?), academia, and even branching out into the public service. I applied to work at a local council. Their rejection confirmed my suspicions: I was not qualified to write parking tickets.

With a few days to go before our self-imposed deadline to leave Melbourne I landed two interviews: one for a job on legendary Australian magazine *The Bulletin*'s website, and one for internet portal ninemsn. Both jobs were based in Sydney, so both interviews would be by phone.

The day for the *Bulletin* interview came. I sat in the front room of the old worker's cottage we had in the suburb of Prahran and tried to be the person they wanted to hire. On the line were editor-in-chief Garry Linnell, editor Kathy Bail, columnist Tim Blair and internet editor Lynda Dugdale. They asked me to rank a bunch of stories in order of importance. My diary notes, 'What a crew … I may have come across as too touchy feely'. I also wrote, 'I have never wanted a job so much.'

It didn't work. Dugdale let me down gently – so gently, in fact, that initially I couldn't understand what she was saying. *The Bulletin* was a publication with a pedigree, a proud history and the big names. As it sank in that I hadn't got the job, I felt like I had been kicked in the stomach.

The interview for ninemsn was different. A bloke called Andrew Hunter and a guy from HR were on the line, and the conference phone kept cutting out. I have always liked the way technical failure screws with expectation. There's freedom in a debacle. I was in the front room again, but I'd read about a trick to make yourself sound more confident: I was standing up. I paced back and forth across the floorboards, expounding my digital news vision. I'd done my homework and I was on the front foot.

In 2006, ninemsn was going strong. The portal had been launched in 1997 as a 50/50 joint venture between Microsoft and PBL Media, the holding company for the Nine television network and ACP Magazines. At the launch party a young, slim-faced James Packer had stood in front of a wall of heavy monitors and declared, 'This is the train leaving the station.'

From launch, ninemsn played a supporting role in most of the big success stories in Australian digital history. SEEK, eBay, realestate.com.au, carsales.com.au: few big sites rose without help from a portal that funnelled all the exit traffic from Microsoft's Hotmail, MSN Messenger and Internet Explorer to one place. Ninemsn was home to all the digital properties of the Nine Network and had the exclusive right to commercialise all the content that came out of ACP Magazines, including *The Bulletin*. For millions of Australians coming online for the first time, ninemsn was the start of the internet. For those in the industry, it was a traffic machine that distributed its bounty with a generous hand.

I got the ninemsn job. It was Andy Hunter who lowered the rope down from the digital chopper and broke me out of my Melbourne predicament. Andy was a big part of why ninemsn had been a success. A powerful mix of consideration and enthusiasm, Andy came first from music – he'd been the bassist in a band called the Daisygrinders – then newspapers, the 'street press' and magazines. He'd done time at ninemsn's main competitor, news.com.au, and had a better grip on digital news than anyone I'd met.

For all the research I had done into the role, and my previous work as a digital editor in the Netherlands, I was pretty clueless. I sat in the ninemsn newsroom in central Sydney, staring at the internet portal's custom-made publishing software and wondering what to do. As Kahneman had discovered 50 years before, vetting officers for the Israeli Defence Forces, my performance in the interview had been no predictor of fitness for the job. Every screen that flashed in front of me looked the same. Here journalists were not reporters or subeditors but 'producers'. What they produced was not stories but 'content'. There was this weird process where you sat down with your manager and talked about yourself. These conversations would begin with 'How are you going?', accompanied by a meaningful look that indicated your psychic well-being was of the utmost importance. A refugee from newspaper culture, I was longing for the reassuring growl of the misanthropic editor and distrustful of an organisation that seemed not so much to observe the world as to collate and package it. There was no perpetually boiling urn, no International Roast and very little foul language.

My breakthrough came with breaking news. One of the commonalities between legacy and digital news media is that other people's disasters are the lifeblood of both. This is not some sick fixation but a reflection of a general truth about people: we need all the information, immediately, particularly if it's about something bad.

Fame, death and a new kind of news

On 4 September 2006 an ambulance press release dropped about a man having been killed by a stingray near Port Douglas in Queensland. This was extraordinary. A few seconds later we learned the unfortunate bloke had been

44 years old. I started writing the first paragraph of the story before the real shock hit. The dead man was Steve Irwin. The Crocodile Hunter was gone.

All my doubts about what to do were dispelled. The death and identity of the victim were confirmed with a phone call while I was still working on that first paragraph. The story fragment was published within seconds, along with a breaking news strap on the ninemsn home page. Traffic to the servers spiked as Australia came online. I proceeded to fill out the story. Unlike in newspapers, my corrections and extensions could be published as fast as I wrote them. Information came in: the ray's barb had gone through Irwin's heart. He'd died almost immediately. His crew had been filming at the time.

Years later, in 2014, the cameraman who was with Irwin finally revealed what happened that day on the Barrier Reef. This was how Justin Lyons described the stingray attack in an interview with Channel 10:

> I remember it very clearly ... we'd been filming with crocodiles and sea snakes – milking sea snakes – and we were looking for tiger sharks on this particular day. We'd had a bit of bad weather, and Steve was like a caged tiger, particularly on a boat, so he said, 'Let's go do something.'
>
> We'd been motoring for a few minutes when we found a massive stingray. We'd swum with stingrays many times before. This one was extraordinarily large – it was eight foot wide – it was very impressive. We were only in chest-deep water. We stood up and chatted about what we were going to do, we made a plan, and slipped into the water.

Stingrays are normally very calm. If they don't want you to be around them they will swim away, they are very fast swimmers ... I had the camera running and I thought, this is going to be great shot, it's going to be in the doco for sure, and all of a sudden it propped up on its front. It started stabbing wildly with its tail – hundreds of strikes in a few seconds.

I panned with the camera as the stingray swam away. I didn't even know it had caused any damage. It wasn't until I panned the camera back [and saw] that Steve was standing in a huge pool of blood that I realised that something had gone wrong.

The stingray barb is about a foot long extending out of the middle of the tail. It's a bit like a fingernail, the other half is embedded in the tail of the stingray ... It's a jagged sharp barb and it went through his chest like a hot knife through butter.

He thought it had punctured his lung, and he stood up out of the water and screamed, 'It's punctured me lung.'

Within a few seconds the inflatable that had been motoring about 30 metres away was there ... He had about a two-inch wide injury over his heart with blood and fluid coming out of it and we thought, we've got to get him back to the boat as fast as we can. As we're motoring back to the boat I'm screaming at one of the other crew to put their hand over the wound. And we're saying, 'Think of your kids, Steve, hang on, hang on.'

He just sort of calmly looked up at me and said, 'I'm dying,' and that was the last thing he said.

Less than an hour after Irwin spoke those words the story broke. The load on the servers – the computers that presented the pages to the public – became unlike anything ninemsn had experienced. They began malfunctioning. Occasionally sites suffer malicious concerted traffic requests, where hackers orchestrate what are called denial-of-service attacks. The news of Steve Irwin's death created an unintentional but massive denial-of-service attack as millions of Australians crammed online. As people saw error pages instead of the story and the technicians began to panic, I experienced a weird sense of peace. The freedom of the debacle. I had landed in the right spot.

From that day, Andy and I and others at ninemsn worked to build a newsroom culture that fused the best of the old with the possibilities of the new. The infrastructure team increased the server capacity, and we made the pages look better, with bigger pictures, headlines and video. We tried hard to be fast and accurate. By far the biggest change for me was the discovery of the audience and the revelation that we could actually see what they wanted to read using software. This discovery fitted hand-in-glove with the commercial needs of our organisation: if we maximised both the number of people looking at our site and how many pages they viewed every time they came, we could make more money. In that era, advertisers were still willing to buy as many banner ads as we could create.

Digital display advertising works by selling standard ad spaces on the page by the thousand. The most common ad is the 'medium rectangle', a piece of desktop real estate 300 pixels wide by 250 pixels deep. Within those 75,000 pixels the advertiser may present any message to the audience there to consume the site's content. A typical CPM (cost per mille, or thousand) of these medium rectangles on an established site would be $10, meaning that for every ad displayed the advertiser pays the publisher just one cent. A single ad displayed once is called an 'impression'.

When you understand the dynamics of the relationship between the publisher and the advertiser, you begin to see why certain things online are the way they are. For example, a publisher may only get one cent for every ad impression, but there is nothing stopping him from loading pages up with multiple ads, thereby increasing the number of impressions every page view delivers. This leads to ad proliferation and cluttered pages. The relationship also encourages the creation of lots of page views. Both of these factors – ad and page-view proliferation – are only relevant so long as the advertiser continues to want the impressions.

That was the game we had been in, the driving commercial force behind the 'pure traffic' era of digital. The problem with this approach was that it was very short-term, flooding the market while compromising audience experience. The push for impressions also came at an editorial cost: the art of the page view slipped easily into an art of darkness.

Running any kind of publication, you are met with the requirement to keep the feeling right, to stay true to your voice while engaging an audience. What Andy and I had found in our modestly sized newsroom was that our devotion to traffic inevitably led young editors to go down dark paths in their daily pursuit of the page view. Digital news outfits publish constantly, with no space constraints, and because of this, maintaining control of voice is more difficult than in a newspaper with a daily deadline. The short-term feedback of the analytical tools shows the site editors what is working, so they obediently 'starve the losers' and then end up with a ghastly news mix. A typical page under this kind of unimaginative regime might feature a foreign murder picture story, with a news lead of a local rape, followed by a sex abuse scandal and a bestiality yarn thrown in for laughs. Sometimes when you challenge a producer on this kind of mix, you see them look at the page as if waking from a dream. They were only doing it for the traffic.

We instigated regulations that limited the number of simultaneous rapes, murders and other gory stories that were permissible on the home page. This eliminated the 'pall of gloom' effect from a story mix that generated traffic but risked leaving the audience depressed and anxious and undermined the long-term future of our site. Bestiality was banned unless there was an overwhelming 'public interest' reason to publish. The in-house style guide specified exactly how much butt-cheek was too much butt-cheek in a thumbnail image.

But we couldn't regulate the problem out of existence. Rules tell you what you must not do – they won't tell you what to create, the vast number of subjects the audience might like but does not yet know about. We needed something – some guidelines, a framework of understanding – that brought science to the process of selecting which of the world's myriad stories we should pay attention to.

Excerpt from the ninemsn Butterfly Bible, *ninemsn 2010*

'"Magic powers": **Mystic beheads toddler, drinks blood'**

Verdict: Unacceptable.

Reason: Too much detail in the headline.

Guideline: Do not treat serious violent incidents with relish. Be particularly aware that violence against children is disturbing to our audience.

'MTV Jackass: **Butt piercing'**

Verdict: Unacceptable.

Reason: Close up detail of buttocks with piercing in progress.

Guideline: Ensure visual decency. Be mindful of your audience.

'Pissed off: **Bible urination behind Hanson's immigration policies'**

Verdict: Unacceptable.

Reason: 'Pissed off' is offensive language used here without a news justification.

Guideline: Ensure written decency. Do not gratuitously cheapen the tone of the home page.

Five years after Steve Irwin's death, news media had transformed again. The power of print had evaporated as audiences went online and changed their daily habits. Many of the old print mastheads still had big audiences, but they were now digital and pulled in less money. Back in 2006, newspapers and magazines had been packed with talent, highly resourced, focused on publishing original content. It was a high-cost set-up. We knew that the kinds of revenues we were making at ninemsn, the biggest digital publisher, would have struggled to fund a newspaper newsroom. What had seemed like bare operating costs for print now looked extravagant.

The Bulletin shut down 18 months after my failed job interview. Everybody was laid off. I went to the magazine's farewell party and realised how much my view of the industry had changed even in that short time. All the people who had interviewed me had been experienced journalists, heavy hitters. Gary Linnell would go on to head up Fairfax. Kathy Bail ended up a publishing CEO. Estimating their salaries based on what I know now, I reckon there was a million bucks of total cost on the other end of that phone line, interviewing a candidate for a minor position. Based on the concentration of cost, maybe I should have been able to predict the fall of the magazine I was then so desperate to join. But in that era, most journalists like me didn't think about the business side of their business. I knew of expensive journalists working for prestigious newspapers who were comfortable filing one story a month. They were doomed.

In digital things were changing too. The pure traffic era was over. Commercially, the market was flooded with ad impressions – prices for excess 'remnant' impressions were dipping below a tenth of a cent – and the audience had tired of Britney Spears and seemed to be moving beyond pure celebrity culture.

Andy and I were sitting around the stone tables in the shade of the Australia Square tower building contemplating what was next. Working with Andy, I'd gone from distrusting anything that didn't look like old newspaper culture – the 'coal face' mentality – to understanding something about technology companies.

The challenging thing about Andy is that he doesn't mind contradiction. Sitting at Australia Square that day, we both agreed it would be good to get some ideas together about the new digital world and publish something. My suggestion was to document what we knew about the art of the page view.

'No, that's the old world,' he said. 'The question is, what's next?'

We sat and watched an ibis circling the tables. When I'd arrived in Sydney, I'd been interested to see these large birds standing on rubbish bins and fossicking in parks. I was amazed when Andy told me they had not always been part of the Sydney city wildlife: 'They weren't around when I was growing up. One day they just appeared.'

I'd imagined the city eternally as I found it. I'd been wrong. Nothing stays the same.

By the time the pungent animal had finished his round, we had our hypothesis about the future of the industry.

Social networks – the platforms that were already sending us thousands of people and growing every day – were going to make news media better.

That day we founded Share Wars – our project to investigate what made news stories share on social networks. The name came from our belief that the social news feeds of individuals would become the next big battlefield for news media, and that the battle would change the nature of the combatants.

> The significant part of [sharing news on social networks] is that it promotes a different kind of feedback loop. It's a feedback loop that stretches out from the individual independent of the publisher, and it's moderated by value. Public value.
>
> It's a channel unlike any the news world has seen before. It will shape not only the way we consume news but also the very stuff of news – the stories themselves.
>
> **From Post 1, Share Wars blog, 4 July 2011**

The new feedback loop between publisher and audience would see news remade in the image of the stories that individuals chose to share. On the whole, that makeover would be an improvement, because people only share what they value.

There were reasons why investigating news on social networks made a lot of commercial sense as well. With the market flooded with dirt-cheap ad impressions, publishers had to try to find a way to prove to advertisers that their content actually meant something to an audience. Getting someone to share a news article, to put their own name and identity to it, represents a deeper commitment than merely getting them to look at it. We reasoned that advertisers would want to be associated with content that was so highly valued by an audience. Sharing indicated true engagement with the content, a trait that could also come in handy in situations where advertisers turned to the publisher for advice on what content would make potential customers pay attention to their message. In Andy's experience, this occurred frequently with big spenders like cosmetics, car and drink manufacturers, who wanted to create bespoke 'hubs' of content they felt suited their products.

Andy and I took our proposal to ninemsn: we wanted to start a private project investigating the drivers of news-sharing on social networks. We decided to pursue a policy of openness with our findings, in the belief that this would create opportunities, but we also wanted to retain ownership. To give over the intellectual property in Share Wars to ninemsn would be signing its death warrant – too many committees, not enough true ownership – and also foregoing any potential commercial value down the track. After some negotiation, our bosses agreed. Newly appointed ninemsn CEO Mark Britt understood that having employees engaged in world-first research could not be a bad thing for his organisation and was unequivocally supportive. Share Wars would remain independent of Australia's biggest internet portal, but we would use the knowledge we gained from the project to help our day jobs. If we discovered the key to news 'virality', we would use it to ninemsn's advantage.

We had our mission. Now we had to pull off the hard bit – gathering the data, studying it, and forming a model for the perfectly shareable story. We never thought that would be straightforward, but neither were we quite prepared for the trip our quest would take us on. We set up a blog and began publishing our ideas on social networks and news.

We knew our message wouldn't be welcomed by many in the media. Not only were we revealing ourselves to be 'demise deniers' and sceptics about the supposed high quality of old media, we were proposing that journalism could be improved by the digital scourge. That message approached sacrilege to journalists in organisations undergoing regular rounds of cost-cutting, who could only see editorial values being undermined.

If you are going to take on the sacred, you'd better have some factual backup. Our first task was to build an engine to harvest the world's news. We would need another Share Warrior: a software engineer.

Chapter 3

The Engine that Share Wars Built

By Domagoj Filipovic

Why do people click the Like button when they read a story? This, of course, was the central question behind the Share Wars project, and my colleagues Andrew Hunter and Hal Crawford had some pretty good ideas.

But ideas are bloody useless.

You see, Andy and Hal's problem was that every Tom, Dick and Harry had their own ideas about why people share stories, but there's very little publicly available data to back up those fanciful theories. Hal and Andy needed to stop writing in the opinion columns and move into the non-fiction aisle. They needed to collect facts. They needed hard data.

This need would drive us to create a piece of software – inspired by a renaissance astronomer – that would go on to kill zombies. A piece of software that had not been seen anywhere else in the world that would drastically change the way we thought about sharing.

This is the story of the engine that Share Wars built.

The notepad and computer

It was a Friday afternoon when I walked into the meeting with Hal.

It was a big meeting room, often used for employee training sessions. There was a large, board-room style table in the middle with seating for 12. Ten computer terminals spanned the long walls, with a projector screen at the end nearest the entrance. The room was called Daiquiri. All the rooms across ninemsn's four floors were named after cocktails, harking back to the carefree early days of the web portal. There was nothing carefree about Daiquiri, though. The room was always freezing due to an air-conditioning fault. Some of the most gruelling meetings in my life had taken place here. Daiquiri was the opposite of rum-drenched good times.

Hal was sitting at the head of the table, his back to the projector screen, waiting for me with his ever-present notepad. Hal and I had previously worked on ninemsn's news and current affairs sites, along with Andy. They were in charge of the editorial team that churned out the stories. I looked after the technical team that built the websites and tools that allowed them to reach their audience.

We hadn't worked together for some time so it was surprising for Hal to call a meeting like this out of the blue.

He told me beforehand that the meeting was to catch up about building something but was thin on detail.

'Hey, mate,' Hal said in his usual welcoming tone.

We exchanged pleasantries and caught up on where we were both at in our respective teams. Hal then began the meeting.

'We've been in the online game for quite some time. We know what works. We know what gets clicks,' he said.

'But we've seen a big shift in the past year or so. Facebook has gone from being a kind of interesting and big web application to being something else entirely, something that has become a really dominant mode of experience for a lot of people on the web.

'As a result, we are seeing a much larger proportion of traffic originating from Facebook and we feel this will change the feeling and the flavour of news.

'We have to investigate. We want to publish something about this but we know we need more substance than just our anecdotes, so we want to build some software that tracks the sharing of news on social networks.'

'How would I go about asking someone to do this?'

Hal laid out the details of his and Andy's plan. They wanted to build some kind of program that would go to the RSS feeds of major news publications and then track how each of those articles gets shared on Facebook and Twitter over time.

RSS feeds are a standard web format that publishes frequently updated information such as news articles, and metadata such as headlines, publication dates and authors' names.

He had piqued my interest. This sounded like a fascinating project from a technical point of view. I let him continue.

'I want to know how I would describe this to a developer. We have a little bit of money that could pay for someone to do it.'

Andy and Hal had done their homework; Hal pointed me to some resource material from people that had started down this path. The building blocks were there, just waiting for someone to put them all together.

I was very excited at this point. This was a fantastic opportunity and I could see exactly how I could put it together. The fundamental architecture was straightforward and made sense. But how could I get in on this project? I proceeded to answer Hal's question directly, keeping my ambition concealed.

'You've got a few options,' I said. 'If you outsource, you'll save on cost but quality will be a risk. You'll need to be very specific with what you want and there could be communication problems.

'You could use a local developer. But that's going to cost you, and I'm not sure that you have enough funds for that.'

I put in a pause and let Hal ponder for a few moments. Now it was time for my offer.

'What if I built you a prototype just to see if this could work? I reckon I could whip something up over the weekend,' I said.

Hal looked up in a sort of expectant surprise. 'Yeah? We'd be happy to work something out in terms of payment.'

'Don't worry about that for now. Let me have a crack at it over the weekend, see what I come up with and we'll catch up next week.'

Hal is a clever man, you see. He is a fantastic people leader and able to inspire in a rare way. He has shown this ability throughout his career. Perhaps it's my own ego talking but I think Hal had been hoping for this result all along.

'How many news sites are we talking about?' I asked.

'Three or four,' he said.

I proceeded to write on my notepad what a high-level set-up would look like. It would have a database at the centre of it. This would do the heavy lifting and data processing. To the left, you would fetch all the RSS feeds from the various news websites. To the right, you would collect statistics from the Facebook and Twitter APIs that make sharing data

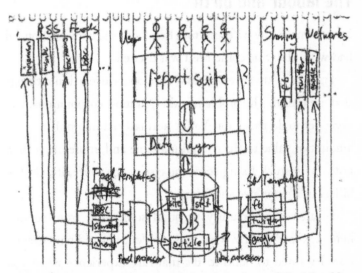

The original 'back of the envelope' architecture of the Likeable Engine from 2011.

public. (APIs – application programming interfaces – define the way in which one website communicates with another). And at the top, you would have a report suite. A simple line chart summarising the sharing trajectory of each article, the 'sharing curve'.

'This is exactly what we want to do,' said Hal. 'Can I get a copy of this diagram?'

'Sure,' I said, and we left it at that.

I had a spring in my step as I walked to the lift. Like a child heading off to Disney World, my imagination was bristling with ideas. I was on a high. I had a weekend to make the ideas in that diagram come to life.

And that is the problem with ideas. They're bloody useless.

The labour and birth

I got home to my wife and told her about the conversation I'd had with Hal. She could see I was excited.

I'm a software developer and developers love to build things that are useful. The problem is that, in most corporations, you don't get to do this a lot. You're normally adding only a small amount of value to the overall machine and, more often than not, you're stuck fixing someone else's code. Sure, it pays the bills, but it's not awe-inspiring.

I had an opportunity to build something from scratch here. I knew exactly what was needed, and I knew exactly how I wanted to build it. It's that rare experience when you feel that you're the king of the world and nothing can stop you.

I started coding the next morning and quickly ran into problems.

There were a million things rushing through my head. What technology would I use? What developer tools should I start with? Was my architecture sound? All of these were important questions to start with, as they would lock in the foundations for the project.

I went with what I had been most comfortable with in my professional career, and that was the Microsoft development stack. I would write the code in C#.NET and the database would be a Microsoft SQL server. I had all the tools and servers on my home computer from personal projects I had done, so we were set up, ready to go.

Next I needed to choose a name for my creation. But what to call it? Hal and Andy were calling their project Share Wars but that didn't feel right. This was something different. I thought about what this 'engine' would be doing. It would be collecting Likes from the social networks. 'Likeable,' I thought to myself. Yeah, that sounded about right. And with a few key strokes, the Likeable Engine was born.

I spent a good 14 hours on that first Saturday engrossed in the code and database. With my headphones on, the world around me disappeared and all I could see in front of me was data structures, algorithms and code.

I kept trying to find the balance between robustness and functionality. This is a trade-off. Any time dedicated to making the software more robust could have been spent building new functionality. It's so easy to get lost and shoot off on a tangent, spending hours on something that turns out to be insignificant in value.

We had adopted the Agile software development process at work, so I decided to use this to keep me on track. I put together a 'backlog' of features and just kept putting them together in order of priority. As I thought of a new feature, I wrote it down, added it to the backlog, prioritised it and, just like that, it was out of my head, allowing me to refocus on the task at hand.

It was 10pm now, and time to sign off for the day. I had successfully got the news processor working. It was able to filter and collect data from news sites. The bottom of the architecture diagram was complete.

My wife had been very patient and had resisted the urge to interrupt all day. 'What exactly are you working on?' she now asked.

I felt like a young child presenting a half-drawn flower on a Mother's Day card.

'This is so good,' I said with puppy-dog excitement. 'I've got the news processor collecting in one thread, and an optimised index for database insertion. I'm using a Singleton to process the requests …' On I went with the technical explanation.

'How good is that?' I asked at the end.

'That's great, Dom. You should be proud of yourself,' she said in the kind of supportive tone that a mother would use on that child with the Mother's Day card.

I could see that she had been lovingly paying attention. But the Likeable Engine was like an iceberg with a missing tip. None of what I had created so far was intelligible to a non-developer.

As much as I appreciated my wife's motherly sentiments, I realised I had work to do. This was still an idea lacking any real substance. I had to re-focus my efforts. Everything below the waterline was in place, but I needed to start building the tip – the data display that would allow Andy and Hal to track the progress of articles being shared in real time.

Overnight sensation

I have always been a good sleeper. Five minutes, and I'm out. Tonight was different. My brain was in overdrive and I couldn't shut it off. It's that feeling you get after you've come home from watching a grand final and you can't stop thinking about the match – only ten times more intense.

I spent the next hour tossing and turning in bed, thinking about the engine. It was nearly midnight and I knew I should get some rest but my brain had other ideas. I went to the study and pushed the computer's ON button. I had to keep going.

The next step was building the chart that would summarise the 'sharing curve'. I had the back end starting to collect data; now it was time to build the top half of the design. I did a quick search for free charting software. After a brief survey, I settled on Google Charts. There was no big reason for this other than that it was Google, so it was bound to have all the features I needed. Right? Wrong!

I quickly found that Google was as useful as lips on a chicken. I don't know if Google Charts has since made improvements, but back in 2011 I had to manually work out where the lines would be drawn on the chart using complex calculations. I'd been hoping that I could just pass the data on to Google Charts and it would work everything out for me but the process was much more complicated than that. Don't get me wrong, I love mathematical problems, but the whole purpose of having charting software is to save you the time and trouble. It should do the heavy lifting for you. Google Charts was nothing more than a glorified image editor.

The next five hours were spent tweaking the chart and getting the data to display correctly. Tapping away at the keyboard, I felt like I was in a movie montage. It was as if the hands of the clock in my study were spinning super-fast and I was speedily forming solutions to problems. I ticked off item after item on my backlog with ruthless efficiency. Everything was flowing effortlessly and I was actually getting results.

It was fascinating to see the data streaming in and the way people were sharing news stories. I was observing this in real time and I was the only one on Earth who was seeing it.

It was a buzz. I was electrified. I was like Steve Jobs on LSD. I could see the future.

I finished the core of the Likeable Engine at 5am and went to bed, exhausted but satisfied. It wasn't perfect by any stretch of the imagination, but it had all the core components. I could now go to Hal and Andy with a prototype. What was more, I'd realised that the idea had legs. It could become a very useful product with real value.

With this possibility in mind, I wanted to ensure that I had some ownership of what I had built. Hal had mentioned payment, but I really wasn't interested in that. I wanted to make sure I wouldn't end up like the Winklevoss twins, the two Harvard alumni (and Olympic oarsmen) who claim that they created Facebook, only to have Mark Zuckerberg whisk it away.'

Likeable meets the family

The meeting with Andy and Hal happened the next day. We were sitting in Australia Square at the same stone tables where Andy and Hal had first conceived the idea for Share Wars. I introduced them to the very first version of the Likeable Engine.

'So there are three parts,' I began. 'To start with, I take some sites (ninemsn, FOXNews.com and nytimes.com, in this case) and I read their RSS feeds and see what new articles they have available. An article is distinctly identified by its URL and all the new ones are added to the database. I continue to do this every 20 minutes or so.

'The second part reads the articles that have been stored and pings [contacts] the Facebook and Twitter APIs. I pass the article URL to the API and it returns the current sharing count (Likes, Share and Comments) for that article. I do this every hour for 24 hours.

'This allows us to show the "sharing curve", how an article trends over the time we are pinging, which is the third part of the Engine.'

'Now, this is just a prototype and needs a fair bit of work to make it more robust, but I hope you get the idea of what it can do.'

GRAPH (LAST 24 HRS TOP 3) [RESET]

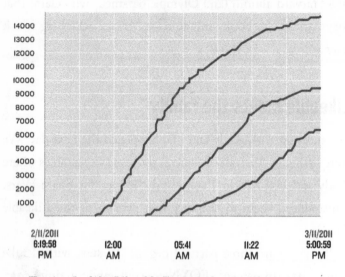

Version 1 of the Likeable Engine, showing the top three
trending stories published globally in the 24 hours from
2 November to 3 November 2011.

'This is great,' said Andy. I could see that he and Hal both
liked it and that it was delivering the core of what they were
aiming for. We proceeded to discuss some more of the details
and how to make the Likeable Engine a part of the Share
Wars project.

'So what would be involved if you built this out for us?'
they asked me.

I felt uncomfortable at this point in the conversation.
What I was really hoping for was that we could form a
threesome, but I didn't know if Andy and Hal felt the same
way. 'Well, for a normal job like this, I'd charge a certain rate
per hour ...'

Andy cut me off at that point: 'Rather than that, how would you like to be the third member of Share Wars?'

'Brilliant!' I thought. We were all on the same page, which was exactly what I'd been hoping for.

'You build the Likeable Engine and we'll use it to validate our theories. If anything comes out of it, we split it three ways'.

And like that, the Share Wars team was complete. Andy and Hal had the journalist background and industry contacts, and I had the technical know-how.

This idea was no longer useless.

But nothing is ever as easy as it seems. I thought I'd have the Likeable Engine completed in a week or two, and Andy and Hal would have their findings shortly after that. Little did I know that we had just started something that would thrust us into the complexities of social networks and reveal things that would flip the conventional wisdom.

Method to the madness

This was now a real project and it was time to build it out properly.

The first task on my list was to determine the sites that we wanted to track. We're talking sites like nytimes.com, dailymail.co.uk, ninemsn and the like. We had originally discussed gathering data from three or four sites, maybe five. I needed a complete list of sites so I could plan how much work would be involved. If it wasn't too much, perhaps I could run this from my home computer.

That's where we ran into the first difficulty.

You see, when you develop a piece of software, you need to make some assumptions. These assumptions form the foundations of a technical architecture and impose certain limitations on future capabilities.

Let me illustrate. Think about a builder constructing a house. The builder needs to know how many storeys the house is going to have so that he can lay the correct foundations to support the structure. If you want a single-storey house, you lay a concrete slab. Go to three storeys and you might dig a little deeper. If you're building a 30-storey high-rise, you'll be doing a lot of excavating. You get the picture?

The email with the list of sites finally came in from Andy. I opened it up.

Sixty-bloody-five websites!

These guys were either crazy or very ambitious, maybe both.

That kind of volume of data meant that I had to completely change my technical strategy. We had only tested Likeable with a few websites. These websites had the same RSS feeds and I had assumed that the RSS feeds for other sites would be the same. Boy, was that a mistake!

While the RSS feed specification is standard, it relies on each website to implement the standard correctly. Unfortunately for us, most sites on Andy's new list had implemented their RSS feeds in slightly different ways.

This introduced a new problem. It meant there would be inconsistency in the data collected.

For example, some sites provided images with their feed, others didn't; some sites included a publication date, some didn't, and of those that did, some were providing the wrong information (a publication date in the future, for example). The feeds were inconsistent and hard to trust.

It was getting complicated. There had to be a better way to collect the data.

Inspiration from the heavens

Nicolaus Copernicus was born on the same day as me, 510 years earlier. That's where the similarities end.

He studied at four different universities in mathematics, painting, astronomy, canon law and medicine. He could speak five languages and the chemical element Copernicum is named after him.

Copernicus published the book *On the Revolutions of the Heavenly Spheres* shortly before his death in 1543. In it, he identified the fact that the sun, rather than our Earth, was the centre of our Solar System. This is common knowledge today, but in the early 16th century, the idea was highly controversial.

Back then, the 'geocentric' (Earth-centred) system was the standard description of the Solar System. And it worked for the most part but had some unnecessary complexities.

If the Earth is the centre of the universe, with the planets and fixed stars revolving around it in uniform circular motions, you should see all the planets move smoothly across the sky at the same pace and with the same brightness. But they don't. The inner planets, Mercury and Venus, never move far from the sun and change radically in brightness. The outer planets move across the sky, then stop, reverse their motion, stop again, then move back the way they were going in the first place.

Much like hard-nosed newspaper editors of yesteryear, astronomers used a combination of witchcraft and gut feel to explain these anomalies. They used things like epicycles and deferents: complex additions to the model to make it all fit. Planets did not in fact orbit the Earth, but another point (P on the diagram), which itself orbited a point some distance away from the Earth (centre of the deferent). This was the usual understanding of the Solar System until the time of Copernicus.

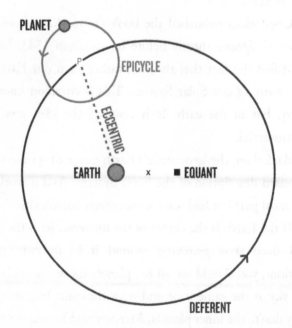

The epicycle and deferent as described in the geocentric model.

So what would compel a learned scholar of the time to question the accepted wisdom? Would you be brave enough to challenge the editor-in-chief?

It all comes down to Occam's razor.

William of Occam was an English Franciscan friar and scholastic philosopher and theologian of the 14th century. The principle that he devised states that when something has two equally plausible explanations, the simpler of them tends to be the likelier. The term 'razor' refers to distinguishing between two hypotheses by 'shaving away' unnecessary assumptions. In other words, keep it simple.

Copernicus knew about Occam's razor and he used it when he saw the complexities of the geocentric system. His understanding of the principle inspired him to shave off the epicycles and deferents and put the sun at the centre. Simple.

The theories put forward by Copernicus were pivotal to modern astronomy and sparked the beginning of a scientific revolution. His birthday was on 19 February, and given that I had this in common with the guy, I thought I might as well make use of Occam's razor as well.

Back to those pesky RSS feeds and their inconsistent data.

How could I solve this problem by simplifying, by using Occam's razor?

What if I looked at the problem from a different point of view? For example, the point of view of the humans who consume the stories?

A typical user would go to a news site and land on the home page. From there they would scan the headlines and click on articles of interest. The home page would provide them with a snapshot of all the stories that were thought to be most interesting.

This was what editors were showing their audiences. This was what they considered to be published content, and they were monitoring their home pages constantly. Don't forget that the RSS feeds were running automatically in the background and could break without anyone knowing. People weren't looking at RSS feeds, they were looking at home pages.

Then it dawned on me: I had been looking at this the wrong way. It should be the *home pages* that I scraped the data from. It's the same thing that Google does to trawl the web. Each page Google hits is scanned for hyperlinks and that's how it finds new content.

I felt like Copernicus coming to the realisation that the sun was the centre of our Solar System. It was the home page that was the centre of our Likeable universe, not the RSS feeds.

If I built a web-scraping template, I could rip all the URLs from the home pages. Only one template was needed for all sites, as each home page code structure was the same. Each was just HTML. Not only that, but with one template we'd be able to add future sites with little effort and the data would be consistent. Perfect for the purposes of scientific analysis. Occam's razor had shorn away the complexities of RSS feeds and replaced them with the simplicity of scraping the home page.

Of course, there was a downside to this approach. We didn't get the exact title of the news story. Instead, we used the link text that an editor provided as the hook for people to click. We felt this was a good enough representation of the real title. We also wouldn't get the exact publication date of the article, but because the Likeable Engine was scanning sites every 20 minutes, we would use the time when we detected the article as a close enough approximation.

RSS feeds could provide this information, but with a lot of added complexity and inconsistency. It was the home-page scrape solution that gave us the key data that we needed, and in the process we gained consistency, simplicity and the ability to add new sites easily.

We were now ready to collect data. Our goal was to set a baseline collection period of three months, after which we would analyse the data.

How Likeable tracks a story

When Analia Bouguet went into labour three months early, it was clear that the child she was bringing into the world was going to face an uphill battle. At birth, Analia's baby girl weighed only 770 grams, and the tell-tale cry was not there. The baby had no vital signs. The situation wasn't looking good.

The medical team at Perrando Hospital in northeast Argentina quickly took the baby away. She was attended to by obstetricians, gynaecologists and a neonatologist. They all reached the same conclusion. The girl was stillborn.

She was taken to the morgue's refrigeration room. Analia Bouguet sobbed in grief as doctors handed her a death certificate just 20 minutes later.

Twelve hours passed and Bouguet and her husband wanted to see their baby's body one last time before leaving the hospital. Bouguet insisted on going to the morgue's refrigeration room with her sister's mobile phone to take a picture of the newborn for the funeral. Her husband opened the drawer and then stepped aside to let her see inside.

She said in an interview with TeleNoticia:

> I moved the coverings aside and saw the tiny hand, with all five fingers, and I touched her hand and then uncovered her face. That's where I heard a tiny little cry. I told myself I was imagining it - it was my imagination. And then I stepped back and saw her waking up. It was as if she was saying 'Mama, you came for me!'
>
> That was when I fell to my knees. My husband didn't know what to do. We were just crying and I laughed and cried, cries and laughter. We must have seemed crazy.

This story broke during our data collection period between 20 March and 20 June 2012 and received a total of 87,000 shares in the first 24 hours.

The Likeable Engine picked up the 'miracle baby' story after it was published on Yahoo! News in the US on 12 April 2012 at 4.51am, Sydney time.

Each time a site is scraped, every hyperlink on the home page is detected and put through a number of checks before it can be added to our database.

One such check is that Likeable compares the links with an ever-growing database, which, at the time of writing, contains over 15 million URLs. If the link already exists, the engine will ignore it because we are already tracking that particular published story. If not, we've found a new article. At this point, the miracle baby story starts its journey in Likeable.

At the same time as the article was inserted into the Likeable Engine, Bouguet named her little girl. She called her Luz Milagros, which means 'Miracle Light'. Luz Milagros was in a critical but improving condition in the same hospital where the staff had pronounced her dead.

'She came out of death, she came out of a drawer and she is in another fight from which she is going to come out again,' her mother said.

The Likeable Engine tracks stories over a 24-hour period. We chose 24 hours because the majority of sharing activity happens in the first day and the story plateaus after that. Likeable holds the stories in a queue that is checked every two seconds to see if the stories have had their hourly check-up with Facebook and Twitter.

Every hour, Likeable contacts the Facebook and Twitter APIs separately and effectively says to them: 'Hey, this miracle baby story. What's the latest share count?' Facebook and Twitter both respond, 'Oh, that one … remarkable story, that. Let me see … it's sharing quite a bit that one, currently sitting at 5000 Likes.'

Oh, if only computers were such animated creatures! If they were, Likeable would note down the response like a good scribe then carry on the conversation for all the other articles in the queue. Alas, that is not the case. All of this happens in code. Ones and zeros travelling along the information superhighway at lightning speed.

At any one point, there are approximately 20,000 articles in the queue and all of them need to be processed. Likeable is making hundreds, even thousands of requests every second for the latest sharing data and so doesn't have the time for idle chit-chat.

People were now talking about the miracle baby. Comments were being re-tweeted. Conversations were starting on Facebook and people were in awe of what had happened after a mother insisted on seeing her baby one last time.

'Follow your instincts, it will never lead you wrong,' said one comment. 'Bottom line, this is a miracle that a mother had her intuition to look one more time. She saved her daughter's life,' said another.

After 24 hours of intense work, Likeable marked the miracle baby story as finished and stopped tracking it. While Luz Milagros began her second chance at life, the 'engine that could' continued on its merry way, scanning all news sites every 20 minutes for new stories to track, while updating the statistics every hour for the stories it was keeping tabs on.

But collecting so much data leaves room for error. What if after the collection period, we looked at the data and realised there were a bunch of things we hadn't taken into account when collecting it?

This fear was realised when we started analysing the data. Out of the shadows would rise a creature that would trouble the Share Wars team for months.

The zombie apocalypse

Big data is big business. Every year, computing giants including Hewlett-Packard, Dell and Cisco sell north of $100 billion in hardware to build server farms around the world.

Facebook itself has so much data that it decided to build its own dedicated server farms. The newest of these lies about 100 kilometres south of the Arctic Circle, in the Swedish town of Luleå. In June 2013, in the middle of a forest at the edge of town, the company opened the mega-sized data centre, a giant building that comprises thousands of rectangular metal panels and looks like a wayward spaceship.

By all public measures, it's the most energy-efficient computing facility ever built: a colossus that helps Facebook process 350 million photographs, 4.5 billion Likes and 10 billion messages a day. While an average data centre needs 3 watts of energy for power and cooling to produce 1 watt for computing, the Luleå facility runs nearly three times cleaner, at a ratio of 1.04 to 1. When you're churning through that much data, it makes sense to build your own super-cooled facility.

With the Likeable Engine now chugging away, we were leeching off this data. We were mining the data-miner.

At this scale, you also start to face all kinds of new problems that you never thought of before. One of them was lurking on our doorstep: the zombie.

Zombies are the bane of a Share Warrior's life. These unnatural stories pop up from the grave with fully loaded

Facebook or Twitter share counts, usually because they were published months or years before the collection period.

Sometimes they are stories that have been re-posted to a forum or message board long after their initial publication and have started to gain traction again.

On other occasions unscrupulous publishers trick the social networks by pointing common content to the same 'canonical' URL. A canonical URL is meant to be used to associate the same content on different websites. A legitimate example might be News Limited running the same article on both the *Daily Telegraph* and the *Courier-Mail* site and using the same canonical. But we found many cases where canonical URLs were used to group content of a similar kind, all quizzes, for example. If you published a new quiz that pointed to the same canonical of all quizzes, you would get a pre-populated share count that had previously accumulated. This is a zombie.

Zombies can and should be dispatched without mercy. They sully the data.

As well as having zombie profiles (see graphic), these stories also seem to have unrealistically big sharing numbers.

Here's an example. In March 2011, a massive 9.0-magnitude earthquake struck Japan, unleashing a terrifying tsunami. The wall of water caused widespread destruction, left about 19,000 people dead or missing and triggered a nuclear crisis at the Fukushima Daiichi nuclear plant.

Australia's ABC News website ran an interactive editorial showing aerial photos over Japan. The before-and-after piece highlighted the devastating effects of the tsunami in stunning

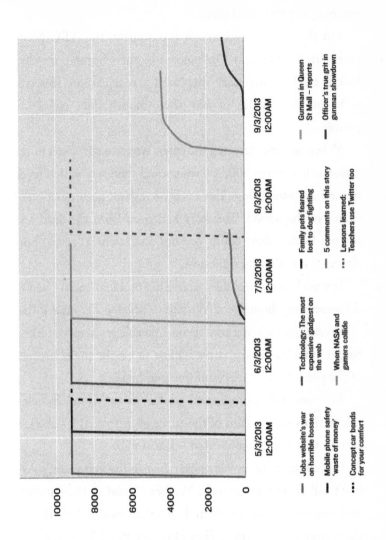

Zombies (the right-angled lines) popping up on version 2 of the
Likeable Engine.

detail. It was one of the most popular articles of the year, reaching over 500,000 shares.

On the first anniversary of the disaster, the ABC News team ran a 'One Year On' piece. On their home page they linked to the same story they used a year earlier. This was right in the middle of our three-month data collection period.

When we first detected the story, we were surprised to see it instantly jump to 500,000 shares and then stay at that level. Something was wrong. There was no organic accumulation of shares in the period. The story had risen from the dead and the pre-loaded share count was not accurately reflecting how the story was sharing right now.

It was clear that zombies were a big problem and we had to do something about them. We had to develop a zombie killer.

When you look at a zombie on Likeable it stands out like a sore thumb. Its sharing curve is close to a right angle, because of the pre-loaded share count (see graphic).

We used this right-angled profile to run some complex calculations on the slant of the curve over time. If it's above a certain threshold, zombie alert – fire at will.

Of course, zombies were never alive in the first place, so we don't kill them permanently. We keep them in the database and continue tracking them like other stories but discard them from our reporting. They never see the light of day.

The fact that zombies were present during our collection period was an important sign. I told you about the size of Facebook's data centre; the amount of data these guys collect is huge and super-complex. We needed to ensure that the data being collected was clean so we could be confident in drawing conclusions, and the zombie killer allowed just that.

Setting free the Likeable beast

The Likeable Engine was made public for the world to use on 27 January 2014. Looking back, we should have launched it on 19 February – Copernicus would have been proud. You can go to http://likeable.share-wars.com and see it in action.

The latest version of the Likeable Engine.

What started off as a three-month experiment for the Share Wars team turned into something that runs continuously for the benefit of the public. Likeable can now be used as a tool to see what the biggest news articles are today and for the past seven days. You can also search by news sites and use particular search terms to narrow your topic area.

During the development of the engine, it became apparent to us that it was not only valuable for our research, but also as a powerful editorial tool. Our graph showed highly shared articles as they rocketed to the top of the sharing pecking order.

The Likeable Engine is unique because for the first time digital media companies don't control the audience engagement data – a couple of social networks do. By dancing with Facebook and Twitter, media companies have accessed a new and substantial distribution pipe, but in doing so have also allowed the social networks to gather and publicly distribute data about them and their audiences. That data was already there, just sitting and waiting to be understood.

Through our research, we discovered how easy it was to access the data and turn it into a pretty and useful graph. For the first time we are able to directly compare the sharing performance of each media company in a completely public and transparent way.

Other organisations such as NewsWhip and BuzzSumo are building businesses around accessing, analysing and presenting similar data.

Journalists from all over the world have started using the Likeable Engine. We didn't expect such broad reach but people were logging on from Australia to Argentina, China to Canada, India to Indonesia. We even had interest from Kenya.

6,192

1

Countries using the Likeable Engine in mid-2015.

During our first three-month collection period, the Likeable Engine collected over 1.4 million articles, with 19 million data points. It had run 24 hours a day on the smell of an oily rag in a web farm in Melbourne. In the end, this was all we needed to get what we wanted from Facebook's chilled mega-server city in Sweden.

The project had been kicked off in the similarly Arctic atmosphere of the Daiquiri meeting room. We had scrawled our ideas on a notepad – the symbol of storytelling – in a room filled with computers – the fusion of inanimate steel, silicon and plastic that had sparked the Information Age. The props of this initial meeting fittingly represented the partnership that gave birth to the Likeable Engine.

Now that we knew what was being shared, it was up to Hal and Andy to examine the stories and see if there was anything about them that could be used to predict their shareability.

Chapter 4

On the Hunt

By Hal Crawford

Nothing says power like a huge chunk of real estate.

Facebook's Menlo Park headquarters sits on San Francisco Bay, taking up 23 hectares of a valley where cottages go for more than a million bucks.

The place used to be occupied by Sun Microsystems and was called Sun Quentin, a play on the San Quentin prison that is also located on the bay. The joke rings true: the complex has a weird vibe. A massive car park surrounds a series of buildings built around a courtyard. It's institutional. Maybe not an exact match for the decaying 19th-century building at the other end of the bay, but enough of an equivalent to give you a sense of oppression. San Quentin State Prison has 4000 inmates, with another 1100 or so guards. Facebook's campus has around the same population – rapidly expanding with the opening of a new, massive building on an adjacent property in 2015. Of course, there's no lethal injection chamber at Facebook. A lot more unplanned collaboration spaces.

As big as this place is, it pales beside the concern it represents. Has any organisation ever boasted so many members? At the start of 2015, 1.44 billion people used Facebook every month. The network founded by Mark Zuckerberg in his dorm room in 2004 has as many devotees as the Catholic Church. It's bigger than India.

It's not the same, of course: the social network is neither a state nor a religion. It doesn't mean as much to people. Another network could rise up to replace Facebook, just as Facebook replaced MySpace. But that's not the point, and in fact, the way we think so lightly of Facebook is one of its strengths. This is a company that legally possesses the personal details and communications of around 20 per cent of the world's population.

That's why I am here, standing in the immense car park at 1 Hacker Way, looking for Building 14, Entrance 2. I want to talk to the people who are using that unprecedented trove of data to understand humanity. Facebook has not been slow to grasp the possibilities: it has been employing serious social networking academics, forming a diverse brains trust the same way you would build up a team of physicists to make a nuclear bomb. It's not the Manhattan Project, but they are up to something. I'm here to find out what.

I locate the building, check in through an iPad, get my adhesive identity badge and sit down. They ask for my name and who I'm here to see, but it would have been just as easy for them to have me sign in with my Facebook ID.

Facebook knows far more about me than any government institution that I can think of. It knows when and where I was born, what I looked like in Year 5, everything about my family, how I relax and what I say to my friends when I've forgotten their birthdays. These are the things I *know* that it knows. *I* did the data entry for them on those facts. When I contemplate all the things I *don't* know it knows about me – through analysis of overlapping data sets and deeper behavioural analysis – I'm overwhelmed. This company can see right through me.

Most social network researchers don't get the opportunity to access that kind of data. They are writing research papers in obscure journals, having surveyed a couple of hundred undergraduates. The difficult language of academia prevents diffusion of their ideas, but there's a deeper problem: they are writing these papers like it's 1999. Like Sun Microsystems is the place to be.

Surely every social network researcher would rather be here, working on the social Manhattan Project with the chance to do experiments on a fifth of the world's population.

One of those lucky enough to be here is Eytan Bakshy, the man I am about to meet. He's part of the Facebook data science team.

Turns out Eytan is short. I can't see him over the heads of the Chinese men who have flooded the small lobby of Building 14. We make for each other through the throng.

I shake his hand.

'How do you pronounce Eytan?'

'a-TAHN.'

We walk through a building that has a deconstructed interior design of visible ceiling pipes and polished concrete. This doesn't feel like Sun Microsystems decor. They had a different flavour of geek culture. We enter a courtyard space with grass and a cycling track marked out like a road. The vibe here is less Sun Quentin and more college campus – if the college had lots of money and the need for tight security.

There is something odd going on in this place, and it involves the gap between what Facebook wants to be and what it is. You see it in the open ceilings and eclectic spaces, the inspiring, counter-cultural things written on the walls. It wants to be the scrappy hacker. It wants to be the college student, earnestly probing the deep questions. But it's not. It's a giant company with billions of dollars in revenue. So when that company asks you, through a message its executives authorised to be sprayed on the wall, 'What would you do if you were not afraid?', it feels jarring. I simultaneously enjoy the implication of universal timidity and find it insulting. I like the question but distrust the questioner – profundity in the service of profit feels weird.

Eytan and I sit down at plastic table under the shade of a tree, and talk social network research. The wind off the bay is cold despite the sun. I work around to my point after we establish that I have read and mostly understood his papers.

'What about the stories?'

'What stories?'

'The things that people are actually sharing on social networks. The content. Have you done work on that?'

Eytan and his colleagues are analysing the network, and they have amazing knowledge of the dynamics of the transfer of information from person to person, but what about the information itself? Why don't they study the content that people are sharing? Doesn't what people actually share mean at least as much as who they share it with? Who's trawling the posts to plumb the depths of humanity?

Eytan's face is framed with hair. Not out of control, but neat all round, a circumference of beard and hair. He is a sensitive man.

'I'm not really a content person. I wouldn't know where to start.'

Caring about the content

That's the kind of sentiment you hear a lot if you spend time with developers or social networking analysts. They divorce the network from what it transmits, or, to put it another way, the platform from the content. It's a powerful approach – one that allows you to 'scale' because the platform is abstract and replicable at low cost. Setting up the infrastructure for Facebook's first member (Zuckerberg himself) might have taken days of coding, but putting on successive members was almost effortless. In fact, by the time Facebook zoned in on its billionth account in 2012, it was scaling so successfully individual members had become difficult to discern.

'Doing data analytics at this scale is a big challenge,' Zuckerberg said when asked if they were going to give the billionth member a prize. 'It's like you're not going to try to pull a billion rows from a database, so you'll pull a sample and project out. I don't know if we knew who the billionth person was.'

Owning a platform makes good business sense. It's what people care about in Silicon Valley. Just as a landlord doesn't get involved in the lives of his tenants, a platform provider doesn't concern himself with whatever the hell the people are doing on his platform. You provide the accommodation and if it works, you're in business. In engineering-based companies like Facebook, Google, Apple and even Microsoft – despite its massive MSN content empire – a robust platform is the goal and anything bespoke is the enemy. Abstraction is a Silicon Valley reflex because the abstract is general and scalable, while things that require work on a piece-by-piece basis are avoided.

Content creation within news media is not particularly scalable. It's one of the things that makes media companies unattractive in the modern business world. Every news story is bespoke – alive with the detail that makes it unique. We could safely ignore the process of creating these stories if they weren't so important to people.

You might think, given that it's their job to create stories, that journalists or journalism academics might have done the work that Eytan and his buddies have not: looking at what content is shared on social networks. This doesn't seem to be the case. For a group whose job it is to be curious, journalists have been remarkably comfortable with not probing into this and many other aspects of their own profession. Instead, the heavy lifting has been left to another group altogether – a group that journalists have been taught to sniff at. It's marketers who understand shareable content best.

From very early days, social networks have been magnets for people wanting to sell things. Marketers don't have the ideological baggage of journalists, so they were swift to see the possibilities of social networks for the promotion of marketing material, and also quick to realise that finally, here was an environment where you could analyse what worked.

What you get as a result is a body of work that has become steadily more insightful about what kind of content is likely to be shared on social media and why.

The SENT factor

I am going to put it on Facebook. I am going to put it on now. What do you do when you find out your friend is being cheated on? I am going to write it on Facebook. I really feel sorry for her. What a bastard. What a fucking bastard. I really do feel like going and strangling him.

I overheard the above in 2014 on one of the commuter train lines that converge on central Sydney like the spokes of a crooked web. A woman in her late twenties was speaking to a friend sitting next to her. By the time I registered the extraordinary conversation, I had missed the beginning. I was dropped into the world of this pair of friends without warning, as were the other commuters around me.

The more I think about the short exchange, the more I realise it exemplifies many of the things that marketers have found out about sharing on social networks.

The first is that the content being transmitted should be **Simple** and immediately graspable.

Secondly, it helps a huge amount if your message is **Emotional**.

Thirdly, it must contain **New information** – this is the core requirement of being interesting, and the more the new information conflicts with a received view of the world, the more interesting it is.

Lastly, something will have **Triggered** or prompted the sharing, and the receiver must have been exposed to it.

These are what I see as the main groupings coming out of the research so far. This scheme of Simple, Emotional, New and Trigger – SENT – is something we coined at Share Wars to summarise other people's findings. The marketers themselves come at things from different angles, some interested in the mechanisms of sharing, some in the motivations of sharers and others in the content itself. They have a lot of recommendations, but if you have the four elements of SENT listed above, you have a very good chance your message will be passed on.

SIMPLE

Most people have had their share of breakups. Almost every adult has experienced the pain of either being dumped or dumping someone, and many have experienced both. For some of us, the pain is a distant memory, for others it's yet to come. Either way, romantic strife is relevant and immediately understandable. It's not double-entry bookkeeping. Everyone gets it. At times this dating game can seem like one vast emotional cage fight from which no one emerges unhurt. Usually the scars are invisible. On the rare occasions when the injuries are physical it gets interesting.

Take the case of Anna Mackowiak and her boyfriend Marek Olszewski. They'd been going out for a few years. This was in Poland back in 2012.

Anna had always been the responsible one, doing what people expected of her, diligent and predictable. To the people she went to school with, Anna had seemed middle-aged, so no one was surprised when she took to dentistry like a duck to water. By her early thirties, she was working in a small dental practice in the city of Wrocław. Then she met Marek. He had been married before and was more than a decade older than her. Sure, people can do what they like. But Marek made her friends feel uncomfortable.

Anna, for her part, was head over heels. Her patients noticed the difference. There was a lightness about her. She was less severe in her advice on tooth care and she smiled often. Then one day the dental nurse found Anna crying in the chair with her phone against her chest. Marek had sent her a text meant for someone else. She'd been betrayed by the first man she'd ever loved; he was having an affair with his ex-wife. While Anna was wrecked, for Marek the situation was completely different. This was a kind of rebirth for him. He was oblivious to the pain he'd caused the dentist from Wrocław. He was so clueless he even came to see her at the clinic, agreeing to a check-up.

'I tried to be professional and detach myself from my emotions,' Anna Mackowiak said later. 'But when I saw him lying there I just thought, "What a bastard," and decided to take all his teeth out.'

Marek was so heavily sedated he didn't realise what had happened to him until he got home and looked at himself in the mirror. His mouth was a bloody mess, and toothless. Anna was hauled in front of the dental authorities.

The story was written up in the local paper, then translated into English and distributed by the Central European News agency. The English-language *Austrian Times* published the wire copy and at some point the story was noticed by the *Daily Mail* and rewritten. The *Daily Mail* story formed the basis of every other English-language version, and there were many. The articles were heavily shared. *The Huffington Post* version, for example, was the 22nd most shared story in the world in a three-month period in 2012. I know, because that's the period when our Likeable Engine first began to collect millions of stories from publications all over the world for analysis.

It's not hard to see why Anna's story did so well. It ticks a lot of the SENT boxes, but the one I want to focus on here is Simple. It's just so easy to grasp. Betrayal is one of the atomic units of human experience. We all need to trust, the cost of trust is the risk of betrayal, and when betrayal happens we understand it immediately.

STICKING WITH THE SCHTICK

Two of the biggest guns in sharing research are brothers Dan and Chip Heath. The Heath schtick begins with picking out some blatantly untrue story that nevertheless refuses to die.

'How many of you have heard the idea we only use 10 per cent of our brain?' Chip Heath asks a group of hotel managers in a training session. 'This is a completely ludicrous, bogus idea. If this were true it would certainly take the fear out of brain injury. You could lose a whole hemisphere and not disturb your ability to do sudoku on the plane on the way home.'

The Heaths go on to show exactly why ideas like '10 per cent brain use' persist. Their 2007 book, *Made to Stick*, is also a great example of its own principles, packed with entertaining stories about what stories are more likely to be shared. The Heath brothers' model of shareable content is the strongest and most wide-ranging marketing-based approach to date, with an emphasis on both factors external to the content and the stuff that is actually baked into it.

The Heath model begins with Simple, which the brothers describe as finding the core of your idea. By definition, the core cannot be 10 things, it has to be the single thing that defines your purpose. Remember that these guys are coming at this from a marketing point of view; they both work in university business schools. They are not news journalists guided by real events. A marketer has a great deal more latitude in what to say. But when you can say anything, what *should* you say?

For the Heaths, the Simple ideal is the proverb, a short saying that illustrates some enduring truth. Take for example the phrase 'A stitch in time saves nine'. It's shorthand for a very sticky piece of advice: you should conduct maintenance now to avoid more expensive work down the line. The important thing about proverbs, apart from their simplicity, is that they feature real, concrete things. This is another part of the Heath model. 'A stitch in time' refers to the mending of seams with needle and thread. It's a real situation. Although sewing is no longer a common skill, clothes are still made of fabric held together with stitches. People know what stitches are.

When you generalise the proverb and take away the particulars – 'Conduct maintenance now!' – you lose most of its power. There's no poetry in the general definition and you have to start using big words like 'maintenance'. I am reminded of the mission statements that supposedly define the purpose and essence of corporations. 'To help make every brand more inspiring and the world more intelligent' is the lofty vision of the Avery Dennison company. There's no hint here of what the company actually does. In its bid to encompass every corporate activity and outcome, Avery Dennison has abstracted its chief activity – making sticky labels – right out of the picture.

This abstraction impulse kills shareability wherever it surfaces. Concrete images – a needle pulling thread, a sticky label placed on an envelope – are easy to remember because they are actual things. General concepts such as 'maintenance' or 'inspiration', for all their utility, are not objects that can be directly pictured in the mind. That makes them difficult to remember and therefore unlikely to be passed on.

This is one of the key messages of the Heath brothers. Find the core of your idea. It will mean making tough choices about what you care about. What is true of the sticky label company is true of everyone: we all have a tendency to lose sight of the main game. Here the classic advice of the experienced journalist to the struggling cadet is relevant: how would you tell a story to a mate at a bar?

Chances are you will be both simple and concrete: a dentist pulled the teeth of a patient; a husband cheated on a wife.

The woman I overheard in the train didn't have to explain why her friend's man's affair with another woman was wrong. It was simple, concrete and clear.

'What a bastard.'

EMOTIONAL

Simplicity alone is generally not enough to make a story 'go viral'. The next element of SENT, Emotion, is where things really get interesting. To illustrate one of the key points around emotion, let me tell you another two stories. They are both about people and they both involve death.

The first story is lovely. Frank Knight was a professional tree-logger who lived in the US state of Maine. In the 1950s, as Dutch elm disease ravaged New England, Frank got into protecting the local trees by removing infected limbs.

One tree in particular he worked hard on protecting. 'Herbie' was the biggest elm in the region, and needed a lot of care. It was old. The seed that became Herbie had germinated in 1793, the same year Louis XVI was beheaded by the French revolutionaries. From then until the mid-20th century, as civil and world wars were fought and empires rose and fell, Herbie grew and flourished in its spot.

Dutch elm disease is caused by a fungus that is spread by bark beetles. These dastardly beetles burrow under the bark, spreading fungal spores. The tree reacts to the infection by blocking the area off with gum, sealing away the fungus and preventing its spread. The tree's own immune reaction becomes the problem, however, because water and nutrients cannot pass the self-imposed blockage and the leaves at the end of those branches die. Eventually the tree ends up shutting itself down completely.

Dutch elm disease is phenomenally potent. It has killed the majority of elms in the northern hemisphere, millions upon millions of trees. There are ways to combat it, but they require a lot of work and care.

That is what Frank gave to Herbie. He kept a lookout for signs of the disease – yellow, wilting leaves – and when he saw them he lopped off the limb. Frank kept up this careful regime for 50 years. It is a well-known psychological tendency to love that which has demanded effort, and keeping Herbie alive had been hard labour. Frank loved the tree. His wife joked that if Herbie had been named Lucy, she would have been jealous.

In 2010 Herbie's immune system won and its last leaves died. The tree was cut down as a public safety measure. Frank died two years later, at the age of 103. Frank's human friends had squirrelled away some of the wood from Herbie and now had it milled into planks. From those planks they built a coffin, and in that coffin Frank was buried.

'I feel like Frank took good care of Herbie. Now Herbie will take good care of Frank,' said a friend. A few versions of the story were written, and the most shared one appearing on Yahoo!

The second story is much shorter.

A Texas father is enjoying a barbecue with his family on his ranch. He hears screams, goes to investigate and catches a friend of the family raping his five-year-old daughter behind a barn. He beats the man to death with his bare hands.

Which story do you think was shared more?

*

Humans are strange animals. Take a perfectly calm man, put him in a lab with no dangers or exciting things around, and tell him a story. Out of nowhere, this guy's pulse races, tiny drops of sweat appear on his hairline, the hairs on his arms stand up. Nothing changed from one moment to the next except those words you told him. That man's body is reacting to story alone. He's ready for action.

In 2011, marketing researchers Jonah Berger and Katherine Milkman discovered something surprising about what puts people in a sharing mood. At the same time as Share Wars was getting underway in Sydney, they were digitally scraping the home page of *The New York Times* to collect stories. They netted 7000 over a three-month period, then separately scraped the *Times*'s 'Most Emailed' story list for the same period. Their question was simple: what stories from the home page made the Most Emailed list and what were their attributes?

'We see that articles that are particularly anger-inducing or anxiety-inducing are more likely to make the Most Emailed list,' said Milkman in an interview with radio program *On The Media*, 'while articles that are particularly sadness-inducing are less likely to make the Most Emailed list.'

For example, a piece titled 'Maimed on 9/11, Trying to be Whole Again' did not crack the list. Milkman was surprised. I am not. The poor disfigured woman of the headline suffered burns to 80 per cent of her body and the article dwells on what she can no longer do.

'I felt like I was young when this happened, and I feel like I'm old now,' says the victim. 'I feel like my past life was a different life.'

Sharing tip: make people mad, not suicidal.

There's a counterweight to the anger and anxiety, though, and this is the surprising part. Berger and Milkman found, along with the bad news, many positive stories. Their highest form was something the pair called 'awe-inspiring', as represented by the news of a discovery of an ancient funeral stone. The stone, or stele, shows a man with a beard sitting at a table with food spread in front of him. It's a scene that could have taken place yesterday in any inner-city hipster cafe, but it's almost 3000 years old. The picture and the writing etched into the basalt are evidence of a belief in a soul separate from the body. The long-dead hipster makes a striking claim in his epitaph: his soul is right there, inside that very stele. Wow.

The thread that runs through both the negative and positive shared stories is the degree to which the story raised emotions that provoked a physiological response. The biggest single driver is emotional intensity, positive or negative. Mild annoyance, contentment, placidity, the wistful: all these gentle things are the enemy of the contagious message.

Now picture this: Jonah Berger, the youthful marketing professor with tight red curls, assembles a group of students for an experiment. He's paying for their time, so he doesn't mind giving them detailed instructions. One half of the group is to stay in their chairs, the other half is to run on the spot for 30 seconds. All the subjects then complete what seems to be an unrelated exercise about a news article and a decision whether to share it or not.

The results come in. The students who jogged are more likely to share, regardless of the content.

Which leaves us journalists, the purveyors of information, in a difficult situation. We want to encourage people to share and we know digital social networks are the best way to do that. We believe that these social networks are hugely important conduits for our work. But the act of consuming our work is almost non-physical. We have brought the physiological requirements of our medium to the lowest levels possible. All you have to do is breathe and move your index finger to click a mouse. With your body in this resting state, your tendency to share is reduced.

We must somehow overcome that. We could make an app designed to be consumed while walking, running or riding a bike. We could focus our efforts on distribution points near the exits of amusement parks. Or we could build an arousal agent into the content itself, a move analogous to building the marketing into the product. The best way to 'activate' the body of someone consuming a piece of news is to make that news emotional. The physiological response is then inextricably meshed with the content – you can't have one without the other.

There are ways of writing and editing that promote emotion, and what we see is that these kinds of appeals to sentiment will be naturally favoured in an environment where social networks provide a large proportion of the audience (see 'Headlines from the Heart' later in the chapter). There are also types of stories that are inherently more emotional – stories about things we care about, like children, animals and our own well-being.

Having been exposed to the research, think about our two examples above – the man who loved a tree and the father who killed in righteous anger. It's easy to guess that the story that more directly connects with our primal survival instincts, our fascination with violence and justice, would be the more shared. Although the beautiful, gentle story of Herbie and Frank was highly shared, it couldn't hold a candle to the Texas Barbecue Slaughter. That horrific tale had a share count six times higher than the good tree-keeper of Maine.

PLAYING THE MAN

Joseph Stalin reputedly said, 'A single death is a tragedy, a million a statistic.' Mother Teresa: 'I can only love one person at a time.' My recent contact with the mysterious Quote Investigator (see Chapter 7) has left me with the feeling that neither of these historical figures said anything of the sort. But the misquotes from the tyrant and saint have resonance because they reflect a universal truth: we relate to individuals, not to numbers. Our pair of friends on the train were not going to post a general moral condemnation of infidelity to Facebook. They were out to expose the 'bastard' who was cheating on their friend. In line with the Simple principle, they were not interested in the abstract, but in the particular, and in line with the second element of SENT, they were engaging emotionally. Telling stories about people is particularly powerful because it tends to satisfy both these elements – Simple and Emotional – at the same time. This principle is no secret the marketers have stumbled on. Newspaper editors and their chiefs of staff have always known it, and a reflex of the news business has been to find an individual who illustrates a particular trend, shift or policy change. A police report on crime increases will result in an assignment to find a mugging victim. If there's been no rain for two years, running the facts from the weather bureau won't do – you need to find the farmer who's shooting sheep.

This traditional emphasis on people stories is backed up strongly in social media: our data shows that of the top 100 shared stories around the world from our three-month collection period in 2012, only 20 were not about personally identifiable people.

Hollywood understands the 'people' principle very well. When Steven Spielberg was casting around in the 1990s for a script to fulfil his dream of making a real World War II movie, he didn't want some balanced and general account of the conflict. He chose a script by Robert Rodat that invented the story of a small group of soldiers looking for another soldier amid the chaos of post D-Day France. A story about individuals. Audiences would not have cared about 'Saving Western Europe' but they flocked to see *Saving Private Ryan*.

Mel Gibson, for all his personal flaws, also has a keen understanding of human motivations. *Braveheart*, which Gibson directed, has been described as one of the most historically inaccurate movies of all time. Pretty much nothing depicted in the film happened or even had a chance of happening in real life. William Wallace, the hero, was not a commoner who fell in love with Isabella of France but an aristocrat who was executed when Isabella was three years old. He didn't wear tartan, he didn't use blue face paint and he didn't rally his troops with the defiant statement 'They may take our lives but they will never take our freedom!'

Audiences don't care. The Hollywood establishment doesn't care. *Braveheart* took millions at the box office, won Gibson an Oscar for Best Director and is credited with reigniting the Scottish independence movement. The emotion evoked by the fictional events in the movie was real, and that emotion went on to have a real impact on the world.

NEW

Let's take stock: so far, following our marketers' recipe for perfectly shareable content, we have a simple and emotional story about people. It's a good start. But there's something missing, something significant, and it goes to the heart of shareability.

Psychologist Daniel Kahneman won his Nobel Prize in economics in 2002, but he only came to truly mainstream fame after he published the book *Thinking Fast and Slow* in 2011.

Journalist Michael Lewis's interview with Kahneman on the writing of this book is full of beautiful insights into a mind tortured by introspection – a mind so aware of its own processes it seems to require a superhuman effort to break through the recursive thinking and create anything. After decades of research and academic publications, and 15 years after the death of his collaborator Amos Tversky, Kahneman collected his findings on the real workings of the human mind in a book accessible to general readers. Even after publication and amidst the world's praise, Kahneman doubted whether he had really nailed it.

'I know it is an old man's book,' he said. 'And now I know why old men write old man's books. My line about old men is that they can see the forest, but that's because they have lost the ability to see the trees.'

Actually it's a wonderful book, full of counter-intuitive insights into the nature of people and how we think. The chief finding is that we use two distinct systems of thought, as indicated by the book's title. 'Thinking fast' is System 1, while 'thinking slow' is System 2.

System 1 is our way of making snap judgements. It operates quickly, without consciousness, and is responsible for a horrifyingly large proportion of the decisions we make. Often decisions made by System 1 are merely ratified by System 2. Kahneman and others have proved that beyond doubt.

System 2, on the other hand, is our conscious thought. It's what we believe we are using most of the time – the plodding and deliberate reasoning that tells us what we are doing is rational. System 2 is real and important, but it is far less effective than we give it credit for being.

Kahneman's explanation of the way System 1 works is fascinating. He says that each of us carries around a detailed mental model of the existing world. It is the job of System 1 to hold that mental model ready for comparison with sensory input. Any input that corresponds with the existing model is let through the system without comment. Nothing to see here. Anything that contradicts the mental model of the world is flagged for the attention of System 2.

This switch when there is a discrepancy – when something does not correspond with our existing mental model of the world – goes to the heart of what makes a news story shareable. New information – information that requires us to think and update our mental model – is the key to gaining and holding the attention of our fellow beings.

The Heath brothers, looking at this from a marketing point of view, say that 'the unexpected' is a key component of shareable content. Jonah Sachs, a marketing theorist who stresses the importance that stories play in the world, says that material should 'be interesting'. These are not glib statements. In Sachs's case, he distils the essence of good advertising into three commandments: Tell the Truth; Be Interesting; Live the Truth. It's a strikingly moral view of the world, and shocking because we expect marketers to be somewhat slick, appearance-before-reality types. In an example of the exact process we are talking about, Sachs gains our attention because his approach is closer to that of the priest than the hustler. His is an ethical set of commandments that serves long-term self-interest.

In fleshing out how to 'be interesting', Sachs focuses on just three human characters: Freaks, Cheats and Familiars. His example of a Freak is Antoine Dodson, the star of what became known as the 'bed intruder' meme. In 2010, the unknown Dodson featured in a local Alabama TV news report about a criminal who had broken into Dodson's apartment and attacked his sister.

'Well, obviously we have a rapist in Lincoln Park. He's climbin' in your windows, he's snatchin' your people up, tryin' to rape 'em. So y'all need to hide your kids, hide your wife, and hide your husband cause they're rapin' everybody out here.'

Sachs points out that Dodson – with his 'sticklike arms' and 'totally unconvincing expressions of menace' – is someone we feel compelled to watch because he doesn't sit easily within our mental models. In contrast, Familiars are those we can relate to in some way and Cheats are those who have contravened important social rules, such as the rule of reciprocation.

Sachs's three characters are a good start – as he says, 'nothing is as interesting to a human being as another human being' – but they don't form a comprehensive description of what makes things interesting. Look at Dodson's statement above and you'll get a sense of the extra layers in the story. It's not just Dodson's character that attracts our attention, it's also the words he uses in his 15 seconds of airtime. They defy expectation. They reverse everything we think we know about serious crime, victims and television reports. They are funny, and funny doesn't normally happen in news stories about rape. This is new information, at odds with our existing world view.

The Heaths also have some great advice on how to be interesting or, as they put it, to create 'the unexpected'. They point to outstanding examples of customer service at the US fashion store Nordstrom: offering free gift-wrapping for presents bought at other stores, helping a customer put snow chains on her car tyres. At some department stores it's difficult even to find a cashier, but a 'Nordie', as the Nordstrom workers call themselves, takes customer service to the extreme. If that happens to you, you have to modify your mental model, and it's worth telling other people about because they too will have to modify some small part of their minds. 'They wrapped ALL my presents!' That makes for effective marketing.

INTO THE GAP

Incompleteness in mental models can be used just as effectively to create interest as discrepancy, something the Heaths point out in *Made To Stick*. Raising a question in the minds of your audience without immediately satisfying it – a technique that forms the basis of storytelling in books, TV shows and movies – is known as creating a 'knowledge gap'. Audiences are remarkably generous with their attention when their desire to know has been aroused; we humans find knowledge gaps so strangely intolerable we will sit through awful crap just to discover 'what happened'. There's nothing more provocative than the 'known unknown'.

Mostly the knowledge gap technique is unavailable to news media. What possible justification could a journalist have for concealing the identity of a murderer until the end of a news report? It's inappropriate, it's not what news is for. The basic rules of news writing dictate that you put the most important facts first and then elaborate; this is what they call 'the inverted pyramid', and it's survived the transition from newspapers to digital news. The writer in this case does precisely the opposite of creating a knowledge gap, instead satisfying the desire to know immediately and providing a few morsels in the afterglow. It would be wrong for a hard-news journalist to tease the audience then reveal important facts at the end of the story. In the case of the first report of a serious car accident, for example, a knowledge gap treatment could involve talking about blood on the road; an ill-fated family outing; a tired truck driver behind schedule; and finally a crash that results in the deaths of two adults and a child.

It doesn't feel right. It's 'too Hollywood', too flippant to play with real people as if they were characters in a screenplay. The audience, the news-reading public, needs to know what happened and why, immediately. It's important not to delay the arrival of that new information at all.

But what happens when the knowledge gap is created naturally? This is a relatively rare situation in news, but when it happens the world takes notice.

A Boeing 777–200ER is 64 metres long with a wingspan over 60 metres. Empty it weighs 145 tonnes; loaded with fuel, people and luggage it's more than double that. If you approach one from the tarmac, the old-fashioned way, the bottom of the fuselage is over your head and the top of the tail five storeys in the air. You could stand inside one of its engines with your arms out wide. It's a big object.

One of these aerial monsters was preparing to fly just after midnight on 8 March 2014. On board, 239 people went about their business: the 12 crew members getting ready for a night's work, the passengers settling down for the red-eye flight to Beijing. They were glad of the plane's air conditioning: outside the night was hot. The airport, dotted with lights, was in the heart of the tropics. Flight MH370 from Kuala Lumpur was about to be cleared for take-off.

The plane roared into the night sky. It flew for 40 minutes, then no one knows what happened. The last radio transmission from the pilot was 'Good night, Malaysian 370,' which sounds creepily like someone saying goodbye to themselves. But signing off with your own flight name is just a standard way for aviators to identify their flights. After that goodbye, the plane went quiet and fell off the air-traffic control radar. The silent aircraft was tracked by military radar as it did a U-turn and flew out into the Indian Ocean. Then it disappeared. Three hundred tonnes of plane and people went missing.

The reaction was electric. Had the plane been shot down? Had terrorists hijacked it? Where was the wreckage? Hanging over all the questions was the general incredulity that a big modern airliner packed with communications technology could simply go missing. Many mobile phones can be tracked via GPS to any point on the Earth's surface, but multimillion-dollar planes don't use that kind of system. Not only did we have to revise our mental models of our technology, but the knowledge gap that was created with the first report of the missing airliner also stubbornly refused to close.

Within 67 days the first MH370 book was published. *MH370: The Mystery* by Nigel Cawthorne is 246 pages long and was written in three weeks. Cawthorne relates the events of the investigation as they occurred, for example repeating the early and incorrect revelation that the pilot's last words were 'Alright, goodnight.' This phrase struck a chord with news editors everywhere but unfortunately doesn't appear on the flight communications transcript. Both Cawthorne and the editors corrected the mistake down the line.

Cawthorne, an amazingly prolific writer who turns his hand to anything that will get him an audience, recognised the potential of the disappearance immediately. I contacted him to ask what he was thinking as he began writing.

He replied: 'Don't think. Just write.'

Here is a guy untroubled by doubt. System 1 all the way. Compare this tabloid-style author churning out books with Zen-like equanimity to the Nobel Prize-winning Daniel Kahneman and his endless self-doubt. Choose your poison.

Cawthorne 'instinctively' knew he had a story on his hands because MH370 closely followed fictional structures that keep people turning pages.

More books about the missing plane followed. There are now well over a hundred, covering the sensible theories and the conspiracy theories and stretching to outright fiction. Screenplays on the missing plane have been written. But whether any of these longer works can match the impact the disappearance had on short-form news media is doubtful: MH370 single-handedly changed the traffic dynamic for news sites in the weeks following its disappearance. Ninemsn saw sustained audience increases of tens of thousands of people throughout March and April.

Cawthorne's book had been out just a month when another Malaysia Airlines plane went down. MH17 was the same model of plane, a Boeing 777–200ER. It was hit by a missile while 10 kilometres above the ground, exploded in the air and smashed into farmland in eastern Ukraine. All 298 people on board were killed. Video of the impact area moments afterwards shows burning debris floating down as villagers look on. There was no mystery, only horror, as the world found out immediately who was dead and why.

Although the destruction of Flight MH17 was big news, it didn't fire the public imagination like MH370. A Google Trends graph shows the term 'MH17' reaching just 60 per cent of the query volume of 'MH370' at the height of its prominence, and the latter flight number generated four times the query volume over the long term. Those reporting the news cannot choose their knowledge gaps, but the two tragedies illustrate the strength of an incomplete mental model. The knowledge gap is one of the most powerful of all ways of presenting information.

For the two women talking on the train, the gap was working in standard fashion: they didn't know when their unfortunate friend would wake up to her predicament. For the listeners such as me, ignorant of the identity of the duplicitous pair, the knowledge gap was working overtime. How would the drama play out?

HEADLINES FROM THE HEART

In February 2014, *Business Insider* ran the news piece 'Facebook Changed How the News Feed Works – And Huge Website Upworthy Suddenly Shrank in Half'.

The news was both true and satisfying to many journalists, as you can tell from *Business Insider*'s headline if you know the first thing about Upworthy: the 15-word, two-clause sentence is a parody of an Upworthy headline.

Upworthy specialises in long, teasing headlines about 'things that matter'. These headlines link to short articles, videos and pictures that frequently fail to deliver on their promise. The 'things that matter' are social justice, racial and sexual equality and freedom, mental illness, the wisdom of children, standing up for yourself, minorities and animals. Three examples:

- '8 love letters to survivors of sexual violence. The one from the dad made me cry.'
- 'Truth time – anyone who's against abortion really should be all for this.'
- 'I thought Alan Cumming had lost his mind, then I watched the video and was so wrong.'

The topics are not what rile most people. It's the style. Upworthy takes its lead from BuzzFeed's approach – personal and full of assumptions. Upworthy is the person at the dinner party who naturally assumes you agree with them. On everything that matters.

ALL YOUR FRIENDS LIKE THIS

The genius of the Upworthy headline is in how it generates an emotional expectation in such a brief format. It deviates significantly from a traditional headline in these ways:

1. Knowledge gaps: every Upworthy headline is an explicit knowledge gap engine that requires a click-through to the article to be resolved.
2. It's long: the typical Upworthy headline is 16 words; a general news website headline comes in under 10. This gives you more space to tell a story with emotional resonance and to create a knowledge gap.
3. Two-part structure: the typical semantic structure of an Upworthy headline is 'A but B'. There is also 'If A then B', 'A then B' and 'A not A' and several others. The two parts give narrative movement to the headline: an achievement in under 20 words.
4. Use of personal pronouns and perspectives: 'you', 'he', 'she', 'me', 'his', 'her' and 'I' feature in around 40 per cent of all Upworthy headlines.

When you throw all these factors into the pot along with an agenda of fighting injustice, you often create something highly shareable. Whether the story lives up to the promise of the headline is a different issue.

Upworthy came out of the blocks at a sprint after its launch in 2012, reaching 88 million people globally by November 2013. In comparison, *The New York Times* reached less than half that many people in the same period. Upworthy was hailed as 'the fastest growing media company in the world'. Then around Christmas 2013, Facebook delivered the present no social network outfit wants: a change in its news feed algorithm. Upworthy traffic declined 46 per cent in two months. Because Facebook doesn't give details about algorithm changes, it's hard to know exactly how Upworthy fell foul of the new rules, but the trend has been a gradual decline ever since. Perhaps the world, and Menlo Park, had their compassion button hammered too many times.

TRIGGERED

So far we have considered some of the key attributes of highly shareable content. Some marketers specialise in an entirely different way of looking at social network sharing. Like Facebook, these analysts prefer to avoid the content of stories and instead focus on more mechanistic examinations of what causes people to share content on social networks. Dan Zarrella, a 'social media scientist', has done a lot of work into simple, quantifiable things like what words you should include in a tweet if you want it retweeted ('you' is the most retweetable word), or what day of the week to post to Facebook in order to get noticed (Saturday).

Zarrella rails against what he calls 'unicorns and rainbows' social marketers: people who make claims without having data to back up any of their statements. One of his points is that if someone isn't aware of and paying attention to your content, he or she can't share it. An observation further to this, and picked up and elaborated upon by Jonah Berger, is that if a story or piece of content never comes to mind, there is no chance it will be passed on. Berger illustrates this by pointing to the breakfast cereal Cheerios, which has a 'word of mouth' score in US households higher than Disney World. People are more likely to talk about a particular kind of cereal than they are to talk about 'the place where dreams come true'? Yes, because everyone eats breakfast every morning. The reality of the mundane trumps the fantastic because mundane is with you all the time. Breakfast cereal is in your face, literally. This kind of physical presentation to your senses is called a 'trigger', and triggers are important if you are a marketer wanting to sell. Triggers also explain why some awful things become overnight sensations.

FRIDAY ON YOUR MIND

Most of the time there are 52 Fridays in a year. Sometimes it's 53. Either way, the incidence of Friday shows a remarkable consistency. It comes around once a week.

Rebecca Black, a 13-year-old from Anaheim Hills, California, had a firm grasp on this regularity when she uploaded her song 'Friday' to YouTube on 10 February 2011. That was a Thursday. As Black points out in the song's lyrics, Friday comes after Thursday, followed in turn by Saturday and ultimately Sunday. That inexorable cycle and the universal good feelings associated with Friday were the themes of what would become known as 'the worst song ever made'. In the first month after Black uploaded it, the video was watched just 1000 times. Then comedian Michael

Nelson sent a link to the song to his 19,000 Twitter followers and it exploded.

The video was watched 167 million times in the space of four months, before it was taken down in a legal dispute. It's back now and has amassed another 70 million or so views.

It is also the second most disliked video of all time on YouTube – 1.45 million people gave it the thumbs down (the most disliked is Justin Bieber's 'Baby'). People hate the song, but they love to hate the song. And while they are loving hating the song, they are entirely susceptible to its trigger. Nelson tweeted his link to the song with the words 'Is this the worst video ever?' on a Friday.

Let's return to our pair of friends on the Sydney train: for some reason, one friend started telling the other something she knew. We've seen that her emotional state would have inclined her towards sharing. She was speaking with real vehemence, and her comment about 'strangling' indicated she was physically activated and ready to share. But that's not the only reason why the pair were having that conversation at that time. There's part of the speech that I haven't yet related. After the woman said, 'I really do feel like going and strangling him …' she went on: 'They catch the train coming in at 6.30 or earlier. They pretend not to be together. They get on at the same carriage and she takes the lid.'

I overhead this 'What a bastard' conversation one morning on my way to work. These friends met each other on the train and sat next to each other, and then one of them was reminded of a story she was burning to tell. It's easy to see why this particular story was brought up in this setting: the 'lid' – the top tier of a double-decker carriage – is exactly where the two women were sitting.

Menlo Park revisited

The world discovered what the Facebook Data Science team was up to in 2014, a year after I met Eytan Bakshy at Menlo Park. Until then Facebook's research had been hidden in plain view: they had been publishing papers and making public statements about their findings. We all knew that Facebook had the data about us that we had given them – birthdates and friends and the names of our first pets. Despite knowing all this, the world hadn't really twigged to the possibilities.

On 2 June 2014, Adam Kramer, the head of Facebook Data Science, published a paper called 'Experimental evidence of massive-scale emotional contagion through social networks' on the prestigious *Proceedings of the National Academy of Sciences* site. In it, Kramer and two co-authors from Cornell University, Jamie Guillory and Jeffrey Hancock, showed that people exposed to less emotionally positive Facebook posts became marginally less positive themselves. A corresponding effect was seen with negative posts. The paper had been a while in the works. The experiment was conducted over one week in January 2012, the paper was submitted late in 2013 and six months later, it was released.

A bit like Rebecca Black's 'Friday', no one noticed at first. The Cornell University media department put out a press release. The first line of the press release reads:

> When it hasn't been your day – your week, your month, or even your year – it might be time to turn to Facebook friends for a little positive reinforcement.

Reading this now feels like watching a dog cheerfully exposing its belly for a nice old scratching. I imagine Cornell was pleased with its snappy release. The research was groundbreaking – for the first time, unequivocal proof on a massive scale of emotional transfer in a social network (online or off) – and it involved Facebook. You get a sense that everyone involved was ready for the praise to roll in.

That wasn't how it turned out. A smattering of specialist sites picked up the news. A pair of Melbourne University academics, Luke van Ryn and Robbie Fordyce, wrote an insightful piece on how the result wasn't quite as significant as claimed.

Then something started rumbling. Four weeks after the paper was published, Robinson Meyer at *The Atlantic* summarised and fuelled a developing social mood: there was something 'off' about the Facebook experiment. Technology campaigner Clay Johnson was one of the most influential critics, tweeting: 'The Facebook "transmission of anger" experiment is terrifying.' Johnson helped Barack Obama win the 2008 US election by masterminding his online campaign. He now advises government on how to deal with social media, and his voice carries weight. Others turned up the dial, describing the Contagion experiment as 'evil' and 'awful'. As the coverage built across mainstream media, academics came out to question first the ethics then the legality of the experiment. The mutt had rolled over and suddenly everyone wanted to kick it.

The researchers' crime had been to take a small fraction of the Facebook user base and adjust the messages these people saw in their news feed, exposing some to less negative and some to less positive friend updates. For example, if I had been in the 'less negative' group and my friend posted 'Friday is the worst song in the world', it might have been removed from my news feed. The impact of not seeing my friend's whine about Rebecca Black's tune was that, statistically, my use of negative words in posts decreased by .07 per cent. That may not sound like much, but to put it in context, the researchers found that in all Facebook posts only 1.6 per cent of words are negative. So something measurable happened, or in this case, didn't happen: I was a happier friend for not seeing the gripe.

In its defence, Facebook pointed out that all the 'censored' posts had been available to view on profile walls, had friends gone looking. But they hadn't asked users for permission, and to this day no one knows who the 689,003 experimental subjects were.

That sounded creepy to a lot of people. I think a lot of the anger came about because people assumed the news feed to be an objective reflection of social reality. It isn't. As any organisation that has lived and died on Facebook traffic knows, Facebook never stops manipulating the feed. To tweak the feed in a way that allowed them to prove something deep about humanity must have felt trivial to the researchers in 2012. It didn't feel that way any more.

Adam Kramer swiftly apologised in a Facebook post: 'I can tell you that our goal was never to upset anyone … In hindsight, the research benefits of the paper may not have justified all of this anxiety.'

The experimenters had shown that emotional states can be transferred, to a very small extent, through written language. They had used Facebook to prove what previously had been impossible to prove, and for their efforts they had a 'fiasco' and a 'PR tailspin' on their hands. The study had revealed what it was within Facebook's power to do, and that unnerved the world.

But the Contagion study, which would go down as one of the company's biggest missteps, is just a small window on the power and possibility. A survey of the Facebook Data Science team's output reveals a bigger, hairier reality.

When I first went to Menlo Park and met Bakshy, he told me of a study in the works that would show how users' political engagement could be altered through what they saw in their news feed. For several years Facebook has been encouraging people to vote in US elections with 'I Voted' badges and other rewards. Being a data-driven company, Facebook measures everything they do, so it is not surprising they tested the effectiveness of the badges by comparing groups of users who saw them with groups who did not. This was an experiment to see whether they could affect voter turnout. They could. By Facebook's own estimation, it induced 600,000 people to vote in the 2010 elections who would not have otherwise done so. In the US, it is well established that higher voter turnout favours the Democratic

Party. Regardless of its motivations, Facebook had in fact influenced the results of an election.

A lot of people were amazed at the scope of the Contagion experiment, and one of the objections was its size: just under 700,000 people. Critics were laying into Facebook for involving so many people in an experiment they had no idea was happening. What was mystifying, as the Facebook and Cornell teams received those hits, was the timing. Why now and not after the other mind-blowing papers they had published over the previous five years? Experiments published before 2014 had bigger samples of Facebook users. A 2013 paper co-authored by Adam Kramer looked at data from 3.9 million accounts. What was astounding about this experiment was how deeply it was able to look into behaviour, running scripts that detected when a user had started writing a post or comment but then stopped. As a result of this ingenious technique, Kramer and his co-author Sauvik Das from the Carnegie Mellon University were able to show that fully one-third of posts were 'self-censored', ending up on the social cutting-room floor. The private behaviour of users in carefully crafting their social personas had been exposed.

Finding love in the numbers

Further indications of Facebook influence are found in a couple of papers published in 2011 and 2012 respectively, concerning the scope and extent of the social network itself. The first is titled 'The Anatomy of the Facebook Social Graph', the second 'Four Degrees of Separation'. Although these papers are descriptions of the network and not experiments, they are written with a certain giddiness as the researchers attempt to convey the breadth of the network and the sheer weight of scientific possibility held in the Facebook servers. Among their most interesting conclusions is the social closeness of the human family. It is overwhelmingly likely that for any person alive today, a friend of your friend knows a friend of their friend. That holds across language groups. We could be talking about a villager in a country on the other side of the world or we could be talking me and you.

'Four Degrees' in particular was given a lot of coverage. But an equally fascinating Facebook Data Science publication was treated flippantly when published in 2013. 'Romantic Partnerships and the dispersion of social ties' describes a way of working out who your wife or husband is from the pattern of your friend network alone. It doesn't sound that spectacular on first pass, but when you get into the details it really is astounding.

The paper, by Facebook's Lars Backstrom and Cornell's Jon Kleinberg, begins with a new way of quantifying connectedness between two people in a network. Normally, networking researchers look at 'embeddedness' between two people to measure network closeness. This is the number of friends they share in common. But Backstrom and Kleinberg came up with a different metric on the hunch that it would tell them something more important about deep ties. They called it 'dispersion', and it is a measure of the 'separateness' of mutual friends.

To put this in a real-world way: say you and I know 10 people in common. How many of these 10 people know each other? If none, that is maximum dispersion. If all know each other, that is minimum dispersion.

So what? Think about the patterns of your social life. Friends tend to be gathered in clumps that correspond to life stages, locations and activities. The people in the 'work' clump all know each other. Same with the people in the 'school' clump. You know all members of both groups but members of the work and school clump are mostly unconnected.

People who are partnered tend to have high dispersion. Remember this is an attribute of two people in a network. You tend to know a couple of people in each of your partner's clumps but you are not 'embedded' in them. The same is true for your partner: he or she connects frugally with groups of your friends who all know each other. As a pair, you have high dispersion.

Now think of yourself as part of a different pair – someone from work, for example. Look at the shape of your shared network. Is it highly dispersed? No. You are embedded with this person, you know a lot of people in common, but all the people you know in common also know each other. You're clumped.

What Lars Backstrom could do, with his unfettered access to Facebook data, was look at the dispersion of anonymous profiles to find the most highly dispersed pairs. He then checked the relationship status field in the Facebook profile for those pairs. More often than not, they were married or in a relationship with each other.

This is the power of Facebook as an experimental tool. Not only does it contain a massive model of real-world social connections, it also has metadata about each network 'node' (profile) that can verify hypotheses based solely on network attributes.

Where I find myself going with Backstrom's work is to infidelity. Take our women on the train. Were they among the 1.3 million Facebook users who the romance experiment took as its extended data set? It's possible. What would the algorithm have seen as it chewed through the network of their deceived mutual friend and 'the bastard'? A couple of blips on the map, connected in a typical pattern that indicates a highly dispersed relationship. In Backstrom's world, the computer has found a partnered couple.

But what if the algorithm went a little further? A little refinement to the calculation that looked for a certain pattern in addition to the dispersion? Take your couple and look for frequent communications between one of the pair and a third profile. The number and shape of the connections in the immediate network vicinity of these three nodes is typical. The trio do not have a lot of friends in common. Possibly there is a history of 'embeddedness' between the third profile and one of the original pair. It's not difficult to imagine, having read Backstrom and Kleinberg's paper, where this is heading. This is an 'infidelity' pattern.

The Data Science researchers could trawl through their millions of records to find these patterns, because they have data on breakups. They can look to see when people change their relationship status to 'single', having been in a highly dispersed relationship. So they know where to look. The data is locked away in Facebook's four massive data centres, three in the US and the one in Sweden.

If you think this is far-fetched, think again: already in the 'Romantic partnerships' paper, Backstrom and his mates showed that a 'less dispersed' relationship was less likely to last, by exactly this technique. Of 400,000 individuals 'in a relationship', those whose partners the researchers could not identify through dispersion were significantly more likely to be single within 60 days.

And if you can do it after the fact – find out who's been cheating on whom and what that looks like in terms of network behaviour – you can do it before the fact. You have the pattern, so why wait for the axe to fall, for your friends to 'put it on Facebook'? Why not receive an alert from the network when it sees something that looks like an unhealthy attachment to a random network node by your loved one? Would people even want a service that could tell them with an 80 per cent probability that their husband or wife is a louse?

I bet that's a question Facebook hopes it never has to answer.

An eerie silence

What it is within Facebook's power to know is unprecedented in human history. Facebook is sitting on the biggest trove of data about the things we value most in the world – ourselves and our relationships – but I get the feeling the company is not going to let its guard down again. The Contagion episode has left scars. As a platform player, Facebook's natural tendency had been not to look 'inside the packet' of the content it distributes, preferring to keep its view at a suitably high level. The minute it went against that tendency, scanning profile updates and posts to determine their emotional tenor, it got hurt. So the shutters have come down. I have tried to get in contact with Backstrom and Kramer to talk to them more about their incredible experiments but have had no response. It seems unlikely I will get back inside Menlo Park.

From the point of view of the Share Wars team, these two broad streams of inquiry into the nature of shareable content – the revelations of the Facebook scientists and the discoveries of the marketers – have hit brick walls. Facebook has gone quiet. The marketers, for their part, want information that will help them help advertisers craft compelling stories that sell their wares. The principles they have discovered – to offer Simple, Emotional pieces of New information – are hugely useful, but the marketing approach diverges significantly from the news approach because of the ever-present advertiser. Marketing, by definition, always has the dual purpose of audience engagement and return on investment (ROI).

Our project – to understand what type of news content gets shared and how that is changing the nature of news publishing – requires a different path. We need to both go further inside the stories themselves and supplement the marketers' SENT approach with another analytical toolkit of our own making.

Chapter 5

When Sharing is Not Sharing

By Andrew Hunter

Things were looking up for Lindsay Lohan mid-morning on 8 June 2012. It was early summer in LA and Lohan was barrelling up the Pacific Coast Highway in her Porsche 911, headed for the set of *Liz & Dick* to play screen idol Elizabeth Taylor.

Lohan had started the year posing as another Hollywood icon – Marilyn Monroe – in a racy shoot for *Playboy*. The issue flew off the shelves. She had hosted *Saturday Night Live* in March, to lead the comedy show to its second-highest ratings of the season. By June the entertainment press was buzzing about her new role as Liz Taylor.

Lindsay Lohan, it seemed, was back.

But she returned with a very high overhead. Lohan disasters had disrupted several productions and the spectre of another catastrophe made *Liz & Dick* almost uninsurable. To finance the film, producer Larry A. Thompson needed to take out 'incarceration insurance'. Lohan's five visits to prison and six to rehab had voided her of second chances. Next time she was going straight to jail.

Lohan also had a serious car-crash problem. Porsches, Maseratis, Mustangs and Mercedes-Benzes had all come to grief while she was at the wheel. *Liz & Dick* producers mitigated this risk with a chauffeur-driven limousine to ferry their leading lady to the Malibu set each day.

Initially the plan worked. For the first three days of filming, Thompson had 'the most insured actress ever to walk onto a sound stage' safely transported to the set.

But for reasons unknown, Lohan chose to drive her 911 to work on day four. It was a decision that would have unfortunate ramifications for many, including a truck driver named James. He was driving an 18-wheeler that Lohan drove her Porsche into.

On the other side of the Pacific, news of the crash soon raced to the top of the most-read lists on Australia's major news websites. The story 'Lindsay Lohan in Bad Car Crash' would receive about 120,000 page views on ninemsn. But the article was shared on Facebook just 44 times – by fewer than 0.04 per cent of the people who clicked on the headline. Its follow-up fared even worse. 'Lohan slightly hurt in US car crash' received zero Facebook shares.

Sharers work as filters

In sharing terms, the Lindsay Lohan story had driven Thelma and Louise-style off a cliff into social oblivion.

How was it that a story could be read so widely yet go unshared?

This gets to one of the key concepts of sharing: sharers are filters. People will only distribute what they value and think their networks will value. The Lohan story was devoid of this sharing capital. In fact, it featured a double whammy of unshareable-ness:

1. Its subject was an overexposed celebrity ...

The Share Wars team knew from our early days comparing audience data that the big page-view-generating names of the past 15 years – Britney Spears, Paris Hilton and Kim Kardashian – are sharing kryptonite. Readers might take a quick peek at Kim Kardashian's latest wardrobe malfunction but they will not share it. We believed this was because readers do not think their networks will value these stories or respect their decision to share them.

People tend to share stories that present their best possible side to friends and acquaintances – articles that, by their sharing, suggest a special knowledge, generosity and wit on the part of the sharer. The antics of Hollywood starlets are generally unhelpful for this type of personal marketing.

2. ... who did what she always does.

We already knew Lindsay Lohan crashed cars. This fact fits squarely within Daniel Kahneman's System 1 thinking, the mental shorthand we use to navigate daily life. System 1's Lohan thumbnail sketch is built on the narrative pillars that she parties, turns up late on set and crashes cars. The Santa

Monica incident adds no new information to that mental picture.

It does not penetrate into System 2 – the logical, conscious thought mode that requires energy and action. Although this story has a violent collision at its core, nothing really happens. No fresh data is added to our 'Lohan file', so we instantly deem it unremarkable and unshareable.

It turns out Lohan and her crumpled Porsche are not alone. The reality is more stories than not go unshared. Many more. Almost two-thirds of the 260,000 news stories the Likeable Engine harvested from Australian news home pages in 2012 received zero Facebook shares. Only 3.2 per cent of stories received 100 Facebook shares or more. These figures would be even starker if we sampled *all* stories produced by news publishers, not just those promoted on the home page. Another study similar to ours, by social news start-up NewsWhip, sampled RSS feeds as well as home pages and found 86 per cent of stories were not shared.

It took us a while to work our way down to these unshared stories because what we found at the top of the list was so fascinating. Until this point, we had figured the main driver of social sharing was the desire to make yourself look good by broadcasting witty, interesting and useful content. We expected to see a whole lot of breaking news and helpful, inspiring stories. But as we pored over the first data batch from the Likeable Engine we realised something else was happening. This was evident in our lists of the top 10 most shared stories from the US, Australia and the UK respectively during this period:

US MOST SHARED NEWS STORIES MARCH TO JUNE 2012

1. Cannibal killer ate victim's brain, heart (*Huffington Post*)
2. Obama backs gay marriage (*Huffington Post*)
3. Beastie Boys co-founder Adam Yauch dead at 47 (*Rolling Stone*)
4. Donna Summer dead at 63 (TMZ)
5. Beastie Boys' MCA dead at 47 (TMZ)
6. Man who fathered 30 kids says he needs a break (Yahoo! News)
7. Naked man eating victim's face killed by police (*Huffington Post*)
8. Tanning booth mom calls arrest a misunderstanding (Yahoo! News)
9. Obama says same-sex marriage should be legal (*New York Times*)
10. Tom Gabel of Against Me! comes out as transgender (*Rolling Stone*)

AUSTRALIAN MOST SHARED NEWS STORIES MARCH TO JUNE 2012

1. School 'failed to get me into law' (*The Age*)
2. 'Dead' boy sits up and asks for water at funeral (*Herald Sun*)
3. Giant Queensland spider devours snake (Nine News/ninemsn)
4. 5.2-magnitude quake rocks Victoria (News.com.au)
5. Strong tremors rock Victoria (*Herald Sun*)
6. Jim Stynes loses brave cancer battle (*Herald Sun*)

7. Dogs put down, owners claim mistaken identity (Nine News/ninemsn)

8. Stay classy! *Anchorman 2* gets the green light (News.com.au)

9. Fury at Anzac Day centenary divisive fears (News.com.au)

10. Single Diggers to lose annual free flights home (News.com.au)

UK MOST SHARED NEWS STORIES MARCH TO JUNE 2012

1. Egypt's plans for farewell intercourse law so husbands can have sex with DEAD wives (*Daily Mail*)

2. Artist turns dead cat into helicopter (*Daily Mail*)

3. Samantha Brick on why women hate beautiful women (*Daily Mail*)

4. Chocolate 'may help keep people slim' (BBC)

5. Once-in-a-lifetime picture shows lightning hit Golden Gate Bridge (*Daily Mail*)

6. Borat anthem stuns Kazakh gold medallist in Kuwait (BBC)

7. Computer files link TV dirty tricks to favourite for Mexico presidency (*The Guardian*)

8. Pills filled with powdered human baby flesh discovered by South Korea (*Daily Mail*)

9. Interactive: gay rights in the US, state by state (*The Guardian*)

10. Unemployed bussed in to steward river pageant (*The Guardian*)

The top UK story turned out to be false but the point of our data capture was not to verify. It was to examine how subject matter drives sharing. Was there a way to take certain story ingredients – say, a troubled Hollywood star and a car crash – and predict whether the resulting article was likely to be shared? To answer this we needed to classify our data.

The marketers say that in order to be shared, a message needs to be a combination of Simple, Emotional, New and Triggered (SENT). This formula is useful, but we needed more. We needed a simple template to allow us to slot stories by category, summarising the audience's reason for sharing. 'Why would someone share this?' we asked ourselves.

THE SHARE WARS NIT MODEL:
NEWSBREAKING | INSPIRING | TEAMING

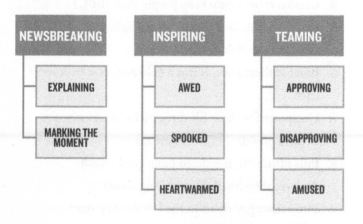

When we sifted through the top Likeable Engine stories across the US, Australia and the UK, three distinct behaviours emerged. We called them Newsbreaking, Inspiring and

Teaming (NIT). For useability's sake, we forced ourselves to choose a single dominant category for each story, despite some crossover.

Newsbreaking is essentially the broadcasting of news. This is the sharer as town crier, announcing the deaths of famous people – musicians Adam Yauch and Donna Summer, and Australian Rules footballer Jim Stynes – or passing on details of an earthquake or police appeal.

Inspiring describes a more traditional notion of sharing: an altruistic, 'here's something special for you' type of distribution. These stories provoke feelings of awe, shock and wonderment. They deal with weird science, mortality, loyalty, triumph over sickness and death, the everyman as hero and amazing children.

The third category is different. 'Obama backs gay marriage', 'Fury over drunken Anzac Day celebration', 'Cyclist kills man after running red light' … these stories are being shared by people invested in issues. The audience is sharing to pass judgement, to take a stand and be seen to be taking a stand. Are you in favour of gay marriage or opposed? How do you feel about Anzac Day? Do you love or hate cyclists? This is sharing that shows what is socially acceptable; that separates wrong from right. This is sharing to define group identity and values. This is sharing that asks, 'Are you for me or against me?'

It was a behaviour, we decided, that was all about teams: defining them and recruiting them. To label this category, we played a favourite trick of Shakespeare's (and more recently the corporate world's) and created a verb from a noun. 'Teaming' was born. Once we'd classified our data, we were surprised to see that Teaming drove almost two-thirds of sharing.

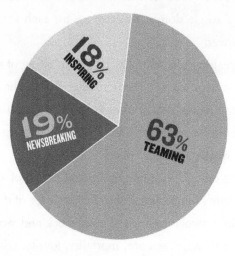

NIT breakdown, Australian news,
March to June 2012.

Sitting under Newsbreaking, Inspiring and Teaming are sub-categories that approximate the sharer's state of mind. Here we asked how the content makes the reader feel. It was a dicey business estimating in retrospect the feelings of people we'd never met, but we had some basic digital forensics to guide us, such as the relative amounts of article Likes and the sentiments of related comments. (This line of inquiry has continued in a project we're conducting with Tim Dwyer and Fiona Martin from Sydney University's Media Department. Part of that investigation involves asking sharers directly why they shared a particular piece of content. For now, however, we have to make do with Likeable data and comment sentiment.)

NEWSBREAKING: SPREADING THE NEWS

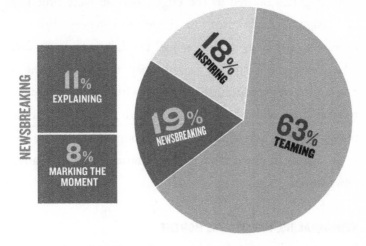

Newsbreaking breakdown, Australian news,
March to June 2012.

NEWSBREAKING: EXPLAINING

Newsbreaking splits into two parts: Explaining and Marking the Moment. Explaining is sharing news to inform or warn. We all have Explainers in our networks – friends who are first to tweet news of an interest-rate cut or details about the earthquake that rocked our suburb 30 minutes ago. This was the sharing impetus behind the top 10 News.com.au story on the Victorian tremor. There is value in this transmission for the sharer (social currency that comes with being in the know) and for the receiver (new information). In this case, News.com.au's story contained important details: the quake's magnitude, the location of its epicentre and eyewitness accounts. Anyone who had felt the quake would have been hungry for information. Those who shared satisfied that need.

As mentioned, the lines between our categories and sub-categories blurred at the edges, but we were brutal in our assignment of stories to a single sub-category. This was necessary to present a clear model for daily newsroom use. Classifying the Victorian tremor story as Newsbreaking > Explaining tells editors that stories with details following natural disasters will be widely shared ... as long they're published straightaway. Explaining accounted for roughly one in 10 shares in our sample of 1000 most shared Australian news stories.

NEWSBREAKING: MARKING THE MOMENT

If you'll permit us a brief detour via New York City's hip-hop scene, the death of a famous musician named Adam 'MCA' Yauch shows why people share to Mark the Moment.

Yauch helped define an era as co-founder of the Beastie Boys, whose hardcore–rap hybrid smashed through mid-1980s pop in a way that foreshadowed Nirvana's ascendancy in the following decade. Before the Beastie Boys, white musicians had only dabbled in hip-hop as a novelty. Rap music was the soundtrack of the black neighbourhoods, as described in Grandmaster Flash's 1982 hit 'The Message'.

That all changed when Yauch and co fused hip-hop and punk in a brash package to inspire a musical mini-revolution. Confounding the critics at first, their debut album, *Licensed to Ill*, would eventually be counted a masterpiece. Its follow-up, *Paul's Boutique*, had reviewers recalling the ground-breaking albums of the psychedelic and prog rock eras. This early work established the Beastie Boys as hip-hop pioneers and their influence and acclaim would roll on well into the new millennium.

In 2012 they were inducted into the Rock and Roll Hall of Fame by Public Enemy's Chuck D, who said it was 'impossible to talk about Jay Z and Eminem without talking about the Beastie Boys'.

Yauch, ill with cancer of the salivary gland, was absent from the ceremony. He released a statement at the time saying he was optimistic about his treatment but was not yet cancer-free. Less than a month later he was dead, aged 47.

In the second half of his short life, Yauch transcended his role as famous musician. He also became a filmmaker and a renowned Buddhist activist who had, in the eyes of many, used his fame to make the world a better place.

'Adam Yauch brought a lot of positivity into the world and I think it's obvious to anyone how big of an influence the Beastie Boys were on me,' Eminem said when his death was made public.

Radiohead's Thom Yorke said: 'We looked up to the Beastie Boys a lot … the Tibetan Freedom Concerts they organised had a very big influence on me personally.'

News of Yauch's death was one of the most-shared topics globally during our 2012 data capture. Of the 1.4 million articles we collected in this period, Yauch stories came in at Number 3 and Number 5 on the US most shared list. This was not a glitch. It was a case of two different stories about Yauch being shared separately on an enormous scale.

Most of the other notable people whose deaths were shared during this period were involved in the arts: the Bee Gees' Robin Gibb, Men at Work's Greg Ham, Booker T & the MGs' Donald 'Duck' Dunn, disco diva Donna Summer, *Where the Wild Things Are* author Maurice Sendak and Marshall amplifiers founder Jim Marshall.

The striking thing about this list is that everyone on it played a part in defining an era through their art (or enabling others' art, in the case of Jim Marshall). Their work scores our memories. Because we associate these people with distinct periods in our lives – pre-school years, disco days, the first time we heard a live electric guitar – nostalgia kicks in when we're alerted to their deaths. We share the news as a tribute. We share to mourn the end of an era or a link to an era passed. We might reflect, even if only momentarily, on the end of our own existence, and so we Mark the Moment. To remember and be remembered.

NEWSBREAKING EXAMPLES

Explaining

- 5.2-magnitude quake rocks Victoria (News.com.au)
- Facebook to acquire Instagram for $1bn (TechCrunch)
- Ben Cousins charged with drug possession (Nine News/ninemsn)
- Earthquake sparks Indian Ocean tsunami alert (*The Australian*)
- Police appeal for help after sausage dog stolen with owner's car (*Courier Mail*)

Marking the Moment

- Beastie Boys co-founder Adam Yauch dead at 47 (*Rolling Stone*)
- Donna Summer dead at 63 (TMZ)
- Rodney King dead (TMZ)
- Jim Stynes loses brave cancer battle (*Herald Sun*)

INSPIRING: SHARING A GIFT

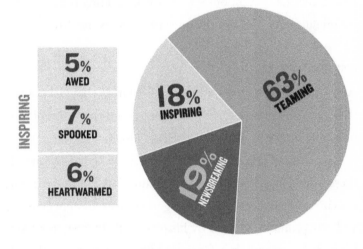

Inspiring breakdown, Australian news,
March to June 2012.

INSPIRING: AWED

Inspiring is sharing to blow minds and break hearts. In the NIT model, Inspiring breaks down into the sub-categories of Awed, Spooked and Heartwarmed. Each contributed about 5 per cent of our 2012 sample's total shares.

Stories classified Awed are often science-based. They almost always provoke a sense of wonder. Sometimes this comes in the face of nature's fury – aerial before-and-after pictures of a tsunami, or an image showing lightning simultaneously striking both arches of the Golden Gate Bridge. This is not Newsbreaking to provide details about a natural disaster. Awed stories shift the focus from information to amazement. They need to be seen to be believed. These are stories that compel us to lift our sights from mundane daily life to the heavens above. When we share news of a discovery of a new nearby planet with Earth-like conditions – when we are sharing the idea that we might not be alone in the universe – awe is the driver.

INSPIRING: SPOOKED

Awed has a close cousin: Spooked. Stories shared because they spook us hint at forces working beyond the realm of our understanding in a way that chills the blood.

The strange tale of Brazilian boy Kelvin Santos is one of these *Twilight Zone* moments. In June 2012, two-year-old Kelvin stopped breathing during treatment for pneumonia and was pronounced dead by hospital staff. His parents took his body home and placed it in a coffin as the family gathered to grieve through the night.

Relatives say an hour before his funeral, Kelvin sat up and asked for a glass of water. Those present thought they were witnessing a miracle. 'Everybody started to scream, we couldn't believe our eyes,' father Antonio Santos said. 'Then Kelvin just laid back down, the way he was. We couldn't wake him. He was dead again.'

The boy was returned to hospital, where doctors re-examined him and confirmed that there were no signs of life. 'They assured me that he really was dead and gave me no explanation for what we had just seen and heard,' Mr Santos said.

Having a child die is the ultimate nightmare for parents. Watching your child die again after seeing what you believed was a miraculous awakening heaps even more pain and shock on the grief. It's a cruel twist.

Sadness is not a strong sharing driver. Berger and Milkman found this, and our data confirmed it. 'No one wants to be "Debbie Downer" in their social network,' says Berger. And he's right. Yet this story's defining element is not sadness but a supernatural weirdness. It provokes meditation on the age-old obsession with life after death. It opens up a knowledge gap of the type Hal described in Chapter 4. Could science explain the boy's final act? Or was it simply a tic or a spasm?

Stories dealing with these types of questions are shared for a distinct reason: they spook us and we think they will spook others.

INSPIRING: HEARTWARMED

The incredible story of Dawn Loggins, a high-school student who triumphed after years of neglect and made it to college, was shared by many thousands because it warmed the heart. The CNN story opens before sunrise as Dawn removes chewing gum from under the desk in one of the classrooms at Burns High School in Lawndale, North Carolina. Dawn is a straight-A student at Burns but also a janitor there. Teachers and residents in her home town got her the job after she and her brother were abandoned by their drug-addicted parents. After years spent growing up in filth, Dawn is unimpressed by the behaviour of some of her fellow students.

'This annoys me, because there's a trash can right here,' she says, removing gum from a desk.

Dawn's off-kilter version of the American Dream is riddled with similar ironic twists. There was no electricity or running water in Dawn's childhood home. Teachers gave her candles so she could do her homework. Dawn and her equally studious brother Shane had to walk 20 minutes to a park to get water for the toilet and to cook with. Dawn would go without showering two to three months at a time and wear the same dress to school for weeks straight.

'Our house was really disgusting,' she told CNN. 'We had cockroaches everywhere. And we had trash piled literally two-feet high. We'd have to step over it to get anywhere in the house. When I was little, it seemed normal to me. I didn't realise that other families weren't living the same way that I was.'

This was a third-world existence right in the heart of the USA. But Dawn and her brother were surrounded by a caring community and teachers who helped however they could, including contributing cash and clothes.

While Dawn was away at an elite natural-science summer program, her parents vanished.

'My grandmother had been dropped off at a local homeless shelter, my brother had just left, and my parents had just gone,' she said. 'I found out later they had moved to Tennessee.'

Dawn was very keen to stay at Burns High School her form teacher asked the school bus driver and the driver's husband to foster the girl for the remainder of her schooling. Other teachers and members of the local community raised money so the young couple could support her. Throughout this incredible ordeal Dawn continued to excel in her schoolwork and finished her final year with a good shot at university. She applied to a number of colleges, among them Harvard, and included a reference from her history teacher. It read:

> I can promise I've never written [a letter] like this before and will probably not write one like this again. Because most students who face challenges that are not even remotely as difficult as Dawn's give up. This young lady has, unlike most of us, known hunger. She's known abuse and neglect, she's known homelessness and filth. Yet she's risen above it all to become such an outstanding young lady.

Months passed and acceptances started to arrive in the mail: big, thick bundles of paperwork accompanied by congratulatory letters. All the North Carolina universities wanted Dawn but she had her heart set on Harvard. Eventually an envelope bearing Harvard's crimson crest arrived. Inside was a letter that read, 'Dear Ms Loggins, I am delighted to report ... that you have been admitted to the Harvard class of 2016.'

Typing 'Dawn Loggins Harvard' into a search engine reveals a continuation of the feel-good story. CNN reported a year later that Dawn had made some good friends and was living in Mark Zuckerberg's old dorm.

The slew of results also shows how Dawn and her teachers inspired hundreds of thousands of others around the world. These are people who have been compelled to put their own troubles in perspective and aim for bigger, better things. They have been moved to share the story so others in their networks will be Heartwarmed too. In doing so they have given their friends something valuable: the gift of inspiration.

INSPIRING HEADLINES

Awed

- Once-in-a-lifetime picture shows lightning hit Golden Gate Bridge (*Daily Mail*)
- Most powerful photos ever taken (BuzzFeed)
- Google tests its augmented reality glasses (*New York Times*)

Spooked

- Giant Queensland spider devours snake (Nine News/ ninemsn)
- 'Dead' boy sits up and asks for water at funeral (*Herald Sun*)
- Giant nine-pound Gambian rats invading Florida Keys (Yahoo! News)

Heartwarmed

- From scrubbing floors to Ivy League: Homeless student to go to dream college (CNN)

- Six-year-old raises $10,000 with lemonade stand (Nine News/ninemsn)
- Deaf boy, 2, hears mum for first time (Nine News/ninemsn)
- 93-year-old woman retires her '64 Mercury (Yahoo! News)

TEAMING: ARE YOU FOR ME OR AGAINST ME?

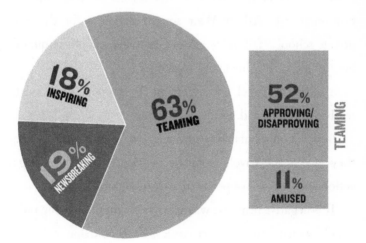

Teaming breakdown, Australian news,
March to June 2012.

What we uncovered next was unexpected. As we examined the data, it revealed most sharing was not transmission for the obvious benefit of the receiver. It was in fact people distributing stories to take a stand on an issue or reinforce group identity: Teaming, in our model.

As soon as we identified Teaming, we started to notice it more in our own social networks. Teamers are people pushing a pet cause: cyclists' rights, pedestrians' rights, anti-fat shaming, environmental and health issues.

TEAMING: DISAPPROVING
Sharing to disapprove of one's fellow human beings is a powerful driver in our NIT model. It was the force behind the most shared Australian story about university student Rose Ashton-Weir, who sued her former school, Geelong Grammar. Ms Ashton-Weir sought damages for the elite private school's 'failure' to educate her well enough to qualify her for law at the University of Sydney.

'I didn't ever feel I was getting the support I needed to really excel,' she said.

Article comments showed readers were incensed by what they saw as the frivolous nature of Ms Ashton-Weir's legal action and her lack of personal accountability.

This negative response was also evident in the sharing ratio, which we used to help sort stories. Facebook shares include Likes, Shares and Comments. Likes are recorded each time a Facebook user clicks the thumbs-up icon. Comments can be registered on the article or in Facebook. Shares are counted when a reader clicks on the Share icon. This action posts an article link with the option of a comment to the reader's Facebook page.

By dividing Likes by total shares and comparing this ratio between stories, we get an indication of whether sharers on the whole approve or disapprove of a story subject. Our assumption is that Likers are Approvers.

In reality, all Teaming stories are shared by both Approvers and Disapprovers. And the ratio is only really useful in identifying overwhelming support or censure. (That's one of the reasons why neither sub-category is broken down in the earlier pie chart.) The lesson for editors is not to try to publish articles that will find comprehensive approval or disapproval but to seek out stories that will compel people to take a stand one way or the other.

However, with a Likes ratio at a low 35 per cent, disapproval of Rose Ashton-Weir appeared to be strong. There were lower counts during our capture period, including Samantha Brick 'on why women hate beautiful women' (17 per cent), 'Mother breast-feeds three-year-old on *Time* magazine cover' (14 per cent) and 'Indonesia bans mini-skirt due to rape link' (12 per cent). These were among the most disapproved of stories in our entire data set. Interestingly, each was about women's identity.

JUDGEMENT DAY

If you regularly share stories about sexism, slut-shaming, parental leave and female body image, you probably read *Daily Life*.

This digital-only Fairfax masthead has flourished during the past few years by focusing on women's issues. It also ranges more widely at times, dealing with such existential knowledge gaps as 'Why do people put those "My Family" stickers on their cars?' Answer: so they appear normal.

Each of the 11 stories *Daily Life* landed in the most shared 500 stories list from February to May 2015 was shared for Teaming purposes. Their stuff is provocative and unapologetic. Readers are almost forced to take sides.

The site's most shared story ever was 'This Is Why You Shouldn't Click on the Naked Photos of Jennifer Lawrence', which yielded a whopping 177,000 Facebook shares and put it into the top 10 most shared Australian stories of 2014.

Editor Candice Chung says it's the forthright approach evident in the Lawrence headline that has driven much of *Daily Life*'s sharing success.

'A lot of our writing is deeply opinionated and it attracts people who like to rally around a cause and like to be seen to rally around a cause,' Chung says.

'With the growth of feminism, and the increase in [awareness of] rape culture and the pay gap, people like to show that they're keen to make a difference.'

The key here for students of sharing is that Teaming behaviour is driven by people not just caring but also wanting to show their network they care.

DAILY LIFE TOP SHARERS
FEBRUARY TO MAY 2015

1. Journalist shuts down interview after man says it's beneath him to be interviewed by a woman
2. Working mothers are the most productive people in the workforce
3. NAB will give new dads 12-week paid parental leave
4. Penny Wong welcomes new baby girl

5. The Reddit question no one should ignore ('When did you first notice men looking at you in a sexual way?')

6. Masa Vukotic murder: travelling alone isn't women's biggest safety risk

7. John Laws, please stop bullying sexual assault victims Why do people put those 'My Family' stickers on their cars?

8. Salvation Army uses #TheDress in powerful domestic violence ad

9. Domestic violence activists call for boycott of *Fifty Shades of Grey*

10. Last Night's *Q&A* tackled our culture of male violence and rape

People are the worst

Among the most despised people in Sharingland are bad parents. Failing what some see as humanity's key biological and social duty – raising defenceless children into well-adjusted adults – is a crime punishable by nasty Facebook comments.

When pictures of Patricia Krentcil first emerged in 2012, it was obvious she had a major problem. Krentcil, a white woman from suburban New Jersey, was the colour of burnt toffee. Her skin was wrinkled far beyond her 44 years. She was a tanning addict who had caramelised herself. But this was not her ultimate crime in the eyes of US news consumers. 'Tan Mom', as she became known, was charged with child endangerment for putting her 14-year-old daughter into a tanning booth. Police were alerted when her daughter showed up sunburnt for school after she'd been 'tanning with Mommy'.

Krentcil denied exposing her daughter to the dangers of tanning but police didn't buy it. Nor did sharers. The judgement of millions on Facebook lifted Krentcil into a stratum of hatred occupied by Nadya 'Octomom' Suleman, the Californian welfare recipient who gave birth to octuplets after in-vitro fertilisation.

Apart from notoriety, these women have something else in common. Their children are seen as victims. Shedding light on the plight of victims is a strong sharing driver. And it is not just human victims that make readers share.

When the story about a Dutch artist, Bart Jansen, turning his dead cat into a helicopter was detected by the Likeable Engine, Hal and I assumed it was being shared by Approvers.

Jansen's 'Orvillecopter' (Orville the cat was named after Orville Wright the aviator) was quite a feat of imagination and engineering.

After having the cat stuffed by a taxidermist, Jansen fixed propellers, stabilisers and remote-controlled electronics to his former pet. Video accompanying the highly shared article about the Orvillecopter shows the cat's carcass stretched prostrate with rotors attached to its four paws. Its bulging dead eyes look straight down the barrel of the camera as its fur ruffles lifelessly in the draft of the rotors. Then it takes off and starts to hover. The camera pulls back to reveal this is taking place in a crowded art gallery. Orvillecopter's 30-something blond, bearded creator flips open a hatch in Orville's back to reveal the cat-copter's electronics. This really is half-cat, half-helicopter.

As jaded news editors, we assumed readers were appreciative of Jansen's creativity and execution. At the time we knew the story was being widely read across the globe. What we realised only after sifting through the data was that Jansen and his Orvillecopter were overwhelmingly disapproved of. Sharers mostly hated the project. A comment from PK in New York on a *Daily Mail* article spoke for many commenters: 'I am a cat lover and I care about all pets. This is no tribute. This is exploitation of the cat to gain attention and feed [Jansen's] narcissism.' Another Disapprover summed up much of the commentary on YouTube: 'Bart, you're perverted but no artist.' To these sharers, Jansen was a deviant. He was Frankenstein in a hoodie.

Deviance and priming

An element of deviance was present in most stories we filed as Teaming > Disapproving. Deviance is perverse, repugnant or criminal behaviour. It was at the heart of *The Huffington Post* story that topped the US most shared list and detailed the horrific crimes of Alexander Kinyua, a 21-year-old Maryland university student who murdered, dismembered and ate his roommate. This was one of a series of 'cannibal killings' reported by US media in the early part of 2012.

The story's timing within this sequence of cannibal killings also contributed to its wide appeal. Readers were primed to share. Priming happens when exposure to stimulus provokes a response in the future. To extend the gun metaphor of Triggered, the fourth part of SENT, priming is the cocking of the hammer. Once primed, the audience is more likely to engage (and share) when Triggered by a reminder or a similar event. Just two weeks before the Maryland murder, former high-school football star Rudy Eugene had walked up to a homeless man named Ronald Poppo in Miami, beaten him unconscious, gouged out his eyes and then chewed off most of his face in an attack lasting almost 20 minutes. Eugene reportedly 'growled' at police before they shot him dead. This episode primed the audience to share stories about the Maryland cannibal.

Both crimes were so bizarre, shocking and perverse as to be almost incomprehensible. Of the Maryland incident, Harford County Sheriff Jesse Bane said: 'This is the first time I can remember … where someone … as part of his crime, consumed the victim.' So this cannibal killing was not standard, in Harford County or anywhere else.

The Share Wars team thought the presence of deviance might drive sharing by creating anxiety in some readers, leading them to examine their own behaviour and test their concept of what is normal. Anxiety is a state of arousal and Berger and Milkman's virality study has shown people are more likely to share media when aroused.

Deviance also compels some readers to reassert their apparent normality within society. By sharing this story about deviant behaviour, they say to their network, 'Look how strange this person is,' and therefore, 'Look how normal I am.' If those within their network agree, group identity is reinforced around this apparent normality. It's doing the same job as those 'My Family' stickers *Daily Life* wrote about. Nothing to see here, folks. Everyone is on Team Normal.

TEAMING: AMUSED

Jumping back to Jansen and his Orvillecopter, it is important to note that the artist and his creation were not universally hated. Some commenters labelled the project 'hilarious!', 'Awesome!' and 'Insane (in a good way)!' For them, Jansen – whose previous creations include the Ku Klux Klock, in which a miniature Klansman popped out of a clock on the hour – was a comic genius. These people were sharing for a different reason. They were Amused. This reader state contributed 11 per cent of shares in our sample.

It was also one of the more contentious aspects of our classification, and the one that generated the most discussion among ourselves. Are people who share content they find amusing really sharing to reinforce group identity?

After poring over the data, we decided the answer was … mostly. In the same way as some people find Jansen's work amusing, some find Will Ferrell's *Anchorman* funny. There is also a whole swathe of humanity that does not 'get it', and it was our contention that people mostly share stories they think are funny to show their networks which camp they're in.

Do you think cannibals are funny? The United States Centers for Disease Control and Prevention (CDC) does.

When the CDC released a statement denying the existence of a virus causing the spate of cannibal killings in 2012, many people were Amused. 'CDC does not know of a virus or condition that would reanimate the dead (or one that would present zombie-like symptoms),' agency spokesman David Daigle told *The Huffington Post*. This is a classic case where the audience shares an in-joke for Teaming purposes. As we know, zombies were hip in 2012. This story came out in the wake of the Miami and Maryland killings. 'Zombie apocalypse' was a high-ranking search term and US TV show *The Walking Dead* was rapidly gaining cult status.

In the week leading up to the CDC's tongue-in-cheek statement, a new cannibal was hitting the headlines. Canadian porn star Luka Rocco Magnotta had been filmed on CCTV in a Paris bar after allegedly mailing a human hand to Canadian PM Stephen Harper. He was also suspected of producing several videos showing kittens being killed, including one that was eaten alive by a Burmese python. Canadian authorities had an even more disturbing video in their possession. This clip showed Magnotta killing, dismembering and eating his boyfriend. 'Imagine the worst horror movie you've ever seen and it's worse than that ... and it's real,' said Montreal Police Commander Ian Lafrenière. 'The murderer just tears the victim apart like a doll.'

Magnotta was a nasty piece of work, possibly a serial killer, according to Canadian police. He was on the run at the time of the CDC's statement. Which begs the question: is this all really funny, or is part of it funny? Can we laugh about a string of attacks this macabre and shocking? Should taxpayer funds go to disease experts confecting statements about the zombie apocalypse? These were the reasons why we classified the sharer's Amused state as Teaming. Effective humour almost always has an edge and works because it says something about those who get it while alienating those who do not. So a team is forged around the funny/offensive material.

TEAMING: APPROVING
Nostalgia for the good old days is often a major Teaming force.

ABC journalist Jonathan Green tapped into this powerful idea when he recalled former prime minister Paul Keating dismantling an ignorant caller to John Laws's radio show back in 1993. Green used the following exchange in a 2012 opinion piece to show how politicians had allowed 'bigots and their mass-media boosters' to hijack public debate since Keating's heyday.

CALLER: Good morning.

JOHN LAWS: Okay, the Prime Minister is here.

CALLER: Yes, good morning. Just a very broad question, Mr Keating, is: why does your government see the Aboriginal people as a much more equal people than the average white Australian?

PAUL KEATING: We don't. We see them as equal.

CALLER: Well, you might say that, but all the indications are that you don't.

PAUL KEATING: But what's implied in your question is that you don't; you think that non-Aboriginal Australians ... there ought to be discrimination in their favour against blacks.

CALLER: I don't say that at all. But my ... myself and every person I talk to - and I'm not racist - but every person I talk to ...

Paul Keating: But that's what they all say, don't they? They put these questions – they always say, 'I'm not racist, but, you know, I don't believe that Aboriginal Australians ought to have a basis in equality with non-Aboriginal Australians'. Well, of course, that's part of the problem.

Caller: Aren't they more equal than us at the moment, with the preferences they get?

Paul Keating: More equal? They were … I mean, it's not for me to be giving you a history lesson – they were largely dispossessed of the land they held.

Caller: There's a question over that. I think a lot of people will tell you that. You're telling us one thing …

Paul Keating: Well, if you're sitting on the title of any block of land in New South Wales, you can bet an Aboriginal person at some stage was dispossessed of it.

Caller: You know that for sure, do you?

Paul Keating: Of course we know it for sure!

Caller: Yeah [inaudible].

Paul Keating: You're challenging the High Court decision, are you? You're saying the High Court got this all wrong.

Caller: No, I'm not saying that at all! I wouldn't know who was on the High Court.

Paul Keating: Well, why don't you sign off, if you don't know anything about it and you're not interested? Goodbye!

Caller: Yeah, well, that's your …

Paul Keating: No, I mean, you can't challenge these things and then say, 'I don't know about them.'

John Laws: Oh well, he's gone.

Keating had a sharp tongue and a fondness for the withering put-down, mostly reserved for those on the other side of politics. 'The thing about poor old Costello is he is all tip and no iceberg,' he said of the Shadow Treasurer at the time. Opposition Leader John Hewson's attack on Keating was dismissed as 'being flogged with a warm lettuce'. He called his successor John Howard 'the greatest job and investment destroyer since the bubonic plague'. He reserved particular scorn for Andrew Peacock, Opposition Leader during the mid-1980s. Keating derided Peacock as unable to 'rise above his own opportunism or his incapacity to lead' and of representing 'nothing and nobody'. When Peacock was having a second tilt at the Liberal leadership, Keating famously quipped that 'a soufflé doesn't rise twice'.

Australian politics has not since seen an entertainer who is Keating's equal, and this makes him even more fondly remembered by his fans. Those who dislike him tend to hate him: a duality that makes Keating an excellent sharing subject. There were – and remain – many Disapprovers of Keating, but the Jonathan Green story, shared on the ABC's opinion site The Drum, was mostly given the thumbs-up. These were sharers publicly declaring their allegiance to Team Keating. That is what Teaming is all about: choosing sides.

TEAMING EXAMPLES

Disapproving

- Cannibal killer ate victim's brain, heart (*Huffington Post*)
- Man who fathered 30 kids says he needs a break (Yahoo! News)

- Tanning booth mom calls arrest a misunderstanding (Yahoo! News)
- Egypt's plans for farewell intercourse law so husbands can have sex with DEAD wives (*Daily Mail*)
- Artist turns dead cat into helicopter (*Daily Mail*)
- Samantha Brick on why women hate beautiful women (*Daily Mail*)

Approving

- Obama backs gay marriage (*Huffington Post*)
- Keating interview highlights the age of the uninformed (ABC)
- Stay classy! *Anchorman 2* gets the green light (News.com.au)
- Tom Gabel of Against Me! comes out as transgender (*Rolling Stone*)
- Interactive: Gay rights in the US, state by state (*The Guardian*)
- 'You're not special' graduation speech sparks buzz (Yahoo! News)

Amused

- CDC denies viral link to zombie killings (*Huffington Post*)
- Borat anthem stuns Kazakh gold medallist in Kuwait (BBC)
- Evil birthday clown stalks your child for a fee (*Huffington Post*)
- Man sings 'Bohemian Rhapsody' in police car after being arrested (Yahoo! News)

Subjects that share

The NIT model categorised sharing by audience motive. Our next analysis was sorting stories by topic. The question here was: 'What is the story about?' Again, this was an assignment of just one subject per story. While many articles are 'about' more than one thing, we forced ourselves to nominate a single primary topic for utility's sake.

Journalists and editors know story subjects go in and out of fashion. We noticed this in the page-view chasing days. Audiences would binge on Paris Hilton for months, until suddenly they couldn't fit any more in. Data from the Likeable Engine shows that the same thing happens with sharing. What shares today might not tomorrow.

Below are the 15 most common subjects from the 500 top-shared Australian stories during our first data capture. The number of stories assigned to a subject is tallied on the x-axis.

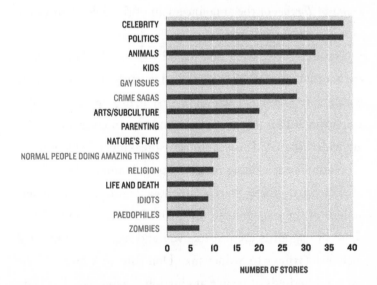

Most shared subjects, March to June 2012.

Dominating the celebrity category in 2012 were two Aussie Rules footballers: Jim Stynes, who died of cancer, and Ben Cousins, who was arrested for drug possession.

This view cut across our NIT model. A Celebrity story might be distributed by readers who are Newsbreaking (Marking the moment of a celebrity death), Inspiring (being Heartwarmed by the actions of a famous person) or Teaming (Disapproving of the lifestyle choices of a star).

Crime sagas capture updates about ongoing police investigations and court cases. The top entries between March and June 2012 were drug smuggler Schapelle Corby's release from jail, the hunt for fugitive Malcolm Naden and the murder of Brisbane mother Alison Baden-Clay. These are shared mostly by Newsbreakers who are Marking the Moment.

Arts/subculture stories are shared by readers Teaming around cult arts subjects such as the release of *Anchorman 2*, *Game of Thrones* or the announcement of the Splendour in the Grass music festival line-up.

Nature's fury during that period was mostly about a small tremor that affected Melbourne and its outlying suburbs. One constant we have noticed since first firing up the Likeable Engine in 2012 is that earthquake and tsunami warning stories are widely shared. This is pure Newsbreaking > Explaining.

Normal people doing amazing things is almost the opposite of Celebrity. These stories are notable for the incredible actions of the protagonists, not their identities ... except that those protagonists are just like you and me. Entries in 2012 included a tribute to Sydney man Don Ritchie, who saved the lives of hundreds of people at cliff-top suicide spot The Gap, and a postman who pulled a stunt on his standard-issue postie bike. This is Inspiring stuff (mainly Heartwarmed and Awed).

Idiots stories are defined by people who do stupid things and shared mostly by readers for Teaming > Amused purposes. Top Idiots in 2012 included a Taliban commander who surrendered in the hope of collecting the $100 reward for his capture, and a motorcyclist photographed tapping out an SMS while riding down the highway.

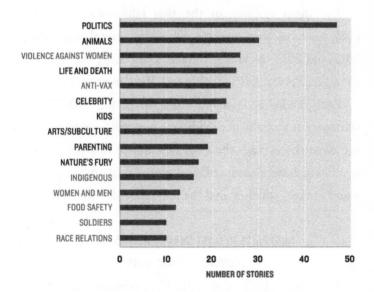

Most shared subjects, February to May 2015.

Repeating this analysis three years later showed that several subjects retained their sharing power. Politics, Animals, Life and death, Celebrity, Kids, Arts/subculture, Parenting and Nature's fury each held their own across the sample periods. Disappearing from view were the Idiots. Zombies completely fell off the radar between 2012 and 2015. Not one Zombie story made the 2015 top 500. Gay issues – mostly gay marriage in 2012 – also slipped out of the top subjects list in 2015. This analysis was made before the Irish referendum and US Supreme Court decisions in favour of gay marriage.

New sharing trends emerging in 2015 included Food safety (dodgy frozen berries and killer onions), Violence against women (physical and sexual assault and the commentary around them) and Anti-vax (debate over the merits of vaccinating children).

The main variable in the two tables was the list of publications we were tracking. We added several sites between 2012 and 2015, including Junkee, Daily Life, the *Australian Financial Review*, SBS, Techly and The Conversation.

Each landed at least one story in the top 500. The real standouts among the new additions were SBS – which earned the most shares with their curious mix of fake and satirical news (which we discounted) and gossip about Asian pop stars – and Junkee, which scored the most shared story.

AUSTRALIA 10 MOST SHARED NEWS STORIES
FEBRUARY TO MAY 2015

1. Today is also 'St Gertrude's Day'; celebrate the patron saint of cats (Junkee)
2. Breaking the cycle: Queensland university student adopts homeless, pregnant teenage cousin (Nine News/ninemsn)
3. Start-up founder cuts $1m salary, doubles staff wages (*Sydney Morning Herald*)
4. Watch the world's first female male model (ABC)

5. Home-grown Derby girl to be town's first Aboriginal doctor (SBS)
6. Dusty the kangaroo thinks he's a dog (ABC)
7. New Zealand war veteran's ANZAC tattoo sparks social media frenzy (Nine News/ninemsn)
8. Katy Perry's 'Left Shark' dancer wins over the internet (SBS)
9. Scholarships in name of Bali duo (*The Australian*)
10. Asian pop: Miss A's Suzy dating actor Lee Minho (SBS)

What's in a headline?

Sharing is a filter for meaning and relevance. Up until this point, our understanding of this filter had come by qualitative assignment of categories and topics. The next step in our sharing quest was to dust off Excel and Likeable's output.

Our method was designed to expose shareable words. First we divided our data set of 260,000 stories into three batches:

1. Those with 100-plus Facebook shares (8000 stories)
2. Those with 1 to 99 Facebook shares (92,000 stories)
3. Those with zero Facebook shares (160,000 stories)

Then we sorted the three lists by headline word frequency using statistics software. Next we deleted all non-nouns but retained personal pronouns and words that are both adjectives and verbs or nouns, such as 'star', 'gay' and 'teen'. We did this to filter the lists for meaning and eliminate unhelpful words such as 'or', 'an' and 'that'. The final step was to delete words that were duplicated across the least shared list and at least one other list. For example, 'man', 'woman' and 'police' appeared in the most shared and most unshared lists. Therefore their presence in headlines did not affect sharing one way or the other.

This is what we were left with:

Most-shared words

1. You
2. Gay
3. Facebook
4. Baby
5. Girl
6. Teen
7. Marriage
8. Mum
9. Life
10. Sex

Least-shared words

1. Stocks
2. China
3. Syria
4. Shares
5. Report
6. Murder
7. Budget
8. Plan
9. Markets
10. Case

Although this was a purely quantitative filter of headline words, it correlated with our subjective topic analysis. 'Gay' and 'marriage' go together, confirming our earlier assessment of gay marriage as one of the biggest issues driving sharing in early to mid 2012. 'Mum', 'baby', 'girl' and 'teen' seem to corroborate the sharing power of parenting.

Conversely, stories with headlines containing the words 'China', 'Syria', 'murder', 'shooting' and 'reports' were disproportionately unshared. We suspected this was because they lacked proximity – and comparative relevance – for an Australian audience. We saw some of these words appear in stories we classified as Newsbreaking and Teaming, just not often enough.

There are some other interesting words to pull from these lists. One is 'Facebook'. We noticed early at ninemsn that stories about Facebook were shared strongly. Research by people like media analyst Dan Zarrella has confirmed that 'Facebook' and 'Twitter' are among the most shared words on their respective platforms. The theory is that communication technologies have an inbuilt promotional advantage.

It's an idea explored by James Gleick in his book *The Information*, which describes the advent in the 1840s of the telegraph – a technology that seemingly radically contracted space and time:

> Information that just two years earlier had taken days to arrive at its destination could now be there - anywhere - in seconds. This was not a doubling or tripling of transmission speed; it was a leap of many orders of magnitude. It was like the bursting of a dam whose presence had not even been known.

Newspapers were eager early clients of telegraph operators. This was despite predictions that the telegraph would render them obsolete because, as one journalist put it, '[Newspapers'] power to create sensations ... will be greatly lessened as the infallible telegraph will contradict their falsehoods as fast as they can publish them.' Instead, editors realised dispatches were more thrilling when slugged 'Communicated by electronic telegraph', and soon the relationship became symbiotic: newspapers provided telegraph operators with revenue, while the telegraph imbued newspapers with a sense of timeliness, as well as a steady supply of stories on its progress and effects. Because the telegraph was an information technology, says Gleick, it served as an agent of its own ascendancy.

There were two forces driving the ascendancy of the telegraph that can also be observed in the growth of Facebook and Twitter.

The first is the network effect – the idea that the network's power grows as more units come online. One fax machine is useless, two machines slightly less useless. But when millions are operating, the network effect exerts a powerful attraction those *without* fax machines. The more fax machines there are, the more there will be.

The second force is the speed with which these technologies have reshaped communication, society and thought. Words and the concepts they describe quickly clashed and melded with the pervasive new technology.

In the case of the telegraph, Gleick writes that this collision 'inspired anecdotes, which often turned on awkward new meanings of familiar terms'. Before the telegraph, people spoke about a message as a physical object. Gleick recounts the story of a US telegraph customer who complained that his message had not been sent because he could still see the paper he had written it on. Then there was the case of the German woman who brought a dish of sauerkraut into the telegraph office to 'send' to her son in a nearby city. Or the story of

John Tawell, a pharmacist from Slough, near London, who poisoned his mistress. After the act, he ran for the train to Paddington, only to be out-raced by the telegraph conveying his description. He was picked up by police and later executed. The story ran in the papers for months. 'Them's the cords that hanged John Tawell,' people would say of the telegraph lines spreading out across the countryside.

Similarly, Facebook has changed the way people interact and think about their place in society. The dominant digital social network has altered the concept of the analogue social network as well as the idea of a 'friend', loosening the definition and spawning the verb 'to unfriend' (a word Shakespeare might have liked). A photo album is now usually a digital artefact. With the advent of Facebook's timeline, your entire adult life is a digital artefact – a record police use as a matter of course in investigations.

Modern society has been intrigued by these details. People have been murdered because they've updated their relationship status to single. Houses have been burned down over unfriendings. Divorce judges have forced couples to hand over their Facebook passwords in order to gather digital evidence of philandering.

The collision of these new platforms with traditional social life creates fascinating storylines that are distributed by the platforms' audiences and by mainstream media. Our analysis of shareable words covered Facebook shares only, so the word 'Facebook' rather than 'Twitter' was shared.

Another interesting word on the least shared list was 'report'. We decided this word was shunned due to its inherent inertia and intentional distance from the action. As a headline device to denote a secondary source, 'report' insulates the publisher from the consequences of inaccuracy. It is often used in headlines of articles rewritten from another publisher's original. For example, 'Lindsay Lohan in car crash: report'. In its other form, as a document explaining or analysing something that has happened or may yet happen, 'report' is devoid of action. News consumers do not warm to inaction. Day-to-day journalism is reactive. There is no story – certainly not one shared by readers – if nothing happens.

That was why we believed sharing would improve journalism. Sharing burns off the abstract and inconsequential. It shows what the audience really cares about. It taps into the fears and aspirations of readers and their networks.

The Lindsay Lohan crash story never got off the launch pad because it was irrelevant, uninteresting and business as usual. There was no harm for website readers in clicking on the story, scanning it for a couple of seconds and moving on to the next thing. But the story was devoid of sharing capital. Those same readers decided their networks did not need to know about the crash, or at least did not need to find out about it from them.

What would have made this story more shareable is a surprise or two – Lohan going against type or doing something else that appealed. Picture this alternative: Lohan rebuilds her Porsche by hand and donates it to the truck driver before vowing to cycle everywhere for the rest of her life.

There are no guarantees of sharing success but that story would have stood a chance. At the very least, Lohan would have had millions of cycling fanatics in her sharing corner.

Chapter 6

The Hard Men of
The Wiggles

By Andrew Hunter

Forget about Team Jacob or Team Edward!! It's Team Sam
or Team Greg!

Facebook commenter Jill Padrotta

Less than 24 hours after dumping lead singer Sam Moran,
The Wiggles arrived at Channel Nine's Sydney studios
unprepared for the polite hell about to be unleashed in the
surprising form of Richard Wilkins.

The plan was to welcome back Moran's replacement –
original Yellow Wiggle Greg Page – play a song and exit the
building.

Only part of that strategy would play out. The interview
would be memorable for other reasons.

There were already warning signs of trouble ahead. Wiggles
HQ had been leaking like Julian Assange. That morning's

newspapers were plastered with grim details from behind the group's white-toothed, wiggly fingered façade. Moran had been called in – leaving his daughter at home on her second birthday – and sacked on the spot, said one insider. Moran was referred to as 'the salaried Wiggle' behind his back, said another. Other reports quoted anonymous staffers lamenting low morale in the organisation.

This was a group who had enjoyed close to unqualified support from Australian media and fans throughout their career. They were national treasures. Now suddenly everyone was sticking the boot in, including the press, and especially the mothers on Facebook:

'It's 1am in UK … wish I hadn't had one last look before bed. Can't sleep now! Devastated!' – Lorraine Speirs.

'Sorry, but I am crying!!! We LOVE Sam the Yellow Wiggle!! DON'T GO!!!!!' – Rachael Howkins.

'Omg I'm shattered!!' – Ashlee Newton.

The reaction was intense, but as The Wiggles sat down with Wilkins on the *Today* set, no one had reason to suspect the Big Red Car's wobbling wheels were about to detach completely.

The skivvy hits the fan …

Wilkins lands the big interviews because he's well connected and can work across the Nine Network's news shows. He also represents a safe pair of hands for nervous celebs. It's not like he's going to skewer you for fun on live TV. But on the morning of 18 January 2012, Wilkins was 'the lad on the spot', as he puts it.

Firmer than usual but charming as ever, Wilkins started asking The Wiggles the questions Facebook wanted answered.

'What about Sam?' Wilkins asked the Blue Wiggle, Anthony Field, whom many blamed for Moran's dumping.

'What about Sam …' an apparently stunned Field repeated to the host. 'Sam was, eh … what do you mean?'

WILKINS: Well, Sam until yesterday was …

FIELD: Yellow … yeah. Well, Sam did a fantastic job for five years, nine years actually … His contract has come to an end … Do we stay with Sam or do we come back to Greg? The energy felt right.

WILKINS: But I guess Sam was an employee rather than full stakeholder in the Wiggles franchise.

FIELD: I have nothing to do with it, Richard …

WILKINS: But Sam was an employee …

FIELD: Sam was doing a job, yeah.

WILKINS: He was a hired hand.

FIELD: Yeah.

WILKINS: I gather this was news to him …

FIELD: Yeah, it was news to him, yeah.

WILKINS: How did he take it?

FIELD: I haven't spoken to him … I don't know.

What was a public relations hiccup before the interview had turned into a social media meltdown. And as The Wiggles took it to the break with a jaunty rendition of 'Toot Toot Chugga Chugga Big Red Car', the mothers of the internet were piling on.

'Watching Channel 9 now with The Wiggles on. Sounds like Sam got screwed.' – Cindy Siekman.

'Shame on you Anthony!!' – Tanya Sanders.

'We can't teach our kids it's OK to use someone … then throw them aside. Outraged!' – Kelly Moate.

'Shame on you Anthony you were my favourite. Your comments on the *Today* show were dismal.' – Alexandra Amalfi.

And that was not the half – or the worst – of it. The shocking force of the reaction was something we have observed repeatedly in our analysis of shared news stories that deal with parents and children. Emotions run high when kids are involved. This sharing behaviour was a classic case of Teaming, mostly by Disapprovers of The Wiggles' decision to sack Moran.

Hello Vera

It would be convenient here to say Wilkins remembers the interview well, but he does not. As I arrive at Channel Nine's low-rise suburban campus on Sydney's North Shore two years later, Wilkins is in the middle of his own social media crisis. He has just referred to singer Aloe Blacc as 'Aloe Vera' on national TV and a small section of the internet is losing its mind.

Wilkins's Nine studio office is full of fantastic memorabilia, including a note from Julio Iglesias that reads: 'Dear Richard, you are always the best and I love you for that … Julio.'

There is a jumble of lanyards and backstage passes next to a Tony Bennett platinum album. On the wall above Wilkins's desk are neat rows of concert tickets surrounded by photos of

Wilkins at various stages of his 30-year career, each seemingly defined by the blondness and length of his mane. A shorter-haired Wilkins smiles alongside Chris Martin of Coldplay. Blonder versions are pictured with Michael Jackson and Julian Lennon. He resembles Jon Bon Jovi in another with a young Kylie Minogue. Russell Crowe has always made time for Wilkins and I spot a photo of them together in black tie.

An official-looking certificate sits above his computer monitor. It is a diploma, from Palmerston North Teachers College, in his native New Zealand. Unexpected.

On his desk is a small samurai sword and three rocks marked 'Gratitude', 'Surrender' and 'Peace'. Wilkins enters his office summoning all three.

I ask him about the Wiggles interview from 2012 and, despite being in Aloe Vera triage mode, he takes the time to watch it on YouTube to jog his memory.

'I think The Wiggles were underprepared and I told them as much,' he says, turning back from his monitor to type on his phone. 'Sorry, I'm being rude.'

His producer Sarah comes in and asks if he wants the message he wrote on Twitter about Aloe Blacc broadcast on Instagram as well.

'Yeah,' he says, turning back to his computer. 'I've got to do a voice for the weekend [*Today*] show's Ozzy Osbourne interview too. [To me] I'm sorry, mate, I've been worried about this immediate disaster.'

His phones are buzzing.

Today host Karl Stefanovic sticks his head in, apologises for interrupting and engages in some charming banter. Wilkins suggests I hang around and then disappears to do a quick spot on *The Morning Show.*

'Are you having a crack at them?' he asks me when he returns. 'I love the guys. I helped launch their first album.'

I suspected Wilkins, who was a pop singer in the early 1980s, might have also known The Cockroaches, the band that spawned The Wiggles. Turns out he did. He remembers them as a 'bouncy, fun bunch of lads' who gigged every night of the week.

Perhaps The Wiggles thought they'd get an armchair ride through the Wilkins interview: a warm welcome back for Greg and a chance to plug tour dates. But there'd been questions to be asked.

'Probably because I've known them for so long ... they weren't prepared for those questions from me, but they should have been,' says Wilkins.

'They should have had something prepared – a good PR spin ... saying, "Look, Sam's a brother. We've toured the world with Sam for the last five years and he's a fantastic guy. He'll always be a Wiggle. Who knows what's in the future, but he's been fantastic and we've loved every second of it. But Greg's back on his feet and we've decided to put the band back together." Full stop.'

The four-skivvy start-up

Manager Paul Field is often cast as the business brains behind the Wiggles machine but insiders say it's his brother's band. Wilkins describes Anthony as 'brilliant', 'a true artist' and 'at the helm of the whole Wiggles creative energy'. There is also a somewhat facetious theory inside the camp that The Wiggles' set-up is Anthony's revenge on older brother Paul, who called the shots in The Cockroaches but has been subject to his younger brother's whims ever since. Anthony himself hints at this in his book *How I Got My Wiggle Back*. '[In] The Cockroaches ... Paul was the lead singer, chief organiser and booker ... and [other brother] John was the main songwriter. I didn't feel I could assert myself.'

Towards the end of his time in The Cockroaches, the youngest Field completed one year of an early childhood education degree and began to harbour a desire to play and record children's music. He suggested to his band mates they do a kids' album, but says in his book that they looked at him as if he were 'completely loopy'. As The Cockroaches wound up, Field resumed his studies at Macquarie University and eventually set up a new band with fellow students Greg Page and Murray Cook and college employee Phillip Wilcher. They played music for kids. When he roped in Jeff Fatt, another ex-Cockroach, to play keyboard, the sound was complete.

'We recorded a bunch of songs and I figured that would be that. But the other guys were quite taken with the idea of our little project becoming a full-time band,' Anthony writes in *How I Got My Wiggle Back*.

The Wiggles would go on to become an Australian entertainment heavyweight, earning more than $300 million during the following two decades.

Success was no accident. Their approach was underpinned by the academic theories of early childhood education. Field would occasionally call on the Macquarie academics to check his approach if one of his ideas was not gelling with the audience. In many ways, they rewrote the rules of preschool entertainment, and these new rules became embedded in the ethos of the organisation as it grew: simple but revolutionary changes such as greeting the audience with 'Hi, everyone!' rather than 'Hi, boys and girls!' There was no room for condescension in their act.

Like The Cockroaches, The Wiggles was a family affair. Paul was recruited to handle the business side of the venture, helping grow the fledgling kids' band into a global phenomenon, while John wrote the songs.

The formula worked, due in no small part to an outward simplicity and positivity that connected with fans across the generations.

But there were problems in Wiggles world. Anthony Field suffered from depression and chronic back pain. At various stages, he overate and became addicted to poker machines. In Page's autobiography, the lead singer also reveals himself as a young man struggling to come to terms with his identity and health for large stretches of the band's career.

Meet the parents

I remember hearing The Wiggles for the first time as a grunge-obsessed 20-something stuck in a car with noisy children. The band immediately had my respect for pacifying the riot in the back seat. Their tunes were catchy enough to have three generations singing along, including someone who preferred Dinosaur Jr to Dorothy.

As a parent 15 years later, I came to appreciate The Wiggles a whole lot more. By this stage, Page had been replaced by Moran, a former understudy. There is a special bond you form as a parent with anyone who can occupy your child for an hour. Our youngest could be plonked in front of a Wiggles DVD and entranced for hours watching Moran, Field and co belt out their stuff. It's cute to watch your child become enraptured by an author or entertainer, and it can't help but rub off on you. My daughter has since moved on and so have I. Now it's all about *Scooby Doo*.

Like many parents on Facebook back in 2012, my wife Rachel and I were fairly well ensconced in Sam's camp when The Wiggles' change in personnel was announced. After all, he'd been lead singer for the past five years, the only Yellow Wiggle our kids had known. In a classic case of Teaming, Rachel changed her Facebook status to 'Team Sam' (although one of her friends thought it was a vote for a troubled werewolf in the TV series *True Blood*).

As a topic, it did not really register on the Share Wars radar at the time, perhaps because the sharing was spread across many articles. Back then we were publishing the top five most shared stories each day on the Share Wars blog, but this included all our international publications, whose share counts generally dwarfed the Aussie sites. Dominating the sharing the day the Moran news broke were stories about a web piracy bill in the US and what went on to become the most shared Australian article of our three-month data collection period: the story of Rose Ashton-Weir, who sued Geelong Grammar.

It was not until May 2012 that The Wiggles made a recognisable dent in the news-sharing universe, at least as the

Likeable Engine measured it. The ninemsn story titled 'Three Wiggles to Retire' scored a healthy 4281 shares, putting it in the top 0.01 per cent of our data set. Trawling through the comments posted at the time provides a taste of the reaction to the news that Page, Fatt and Cook all announced their retirements just three months after Moran was shown the door. Teaming was at work again.

'What a joke. After being so disrespectful to Sam only months ago and kicking him out saying he was only a "hired hand", they've decided to retire and get new blood in. Why the hell couldn't they have sorted this out four months ago and not trashed their reputation???' – Jon.

'Why on earth would they dump the young guy [Sam] when they were going to consider further line-up changes? Doesn't make any sense!' – MC.

Some commenters approved of the move – particularly the decision to make the new Yellow Wiggle a female, Emma Watkins.

'So many haters, but wow, a female Wiggle. I don't know about anyone else, but I find that rather awesome. Go, Emma, and good luck!' – Emma, Victoria.

Sam has his say

Called into the office on his holidays, Yellow Wiggle Sam Moran was relaxed and disarmed – unprepared.

Sporting the kind of facial hair which usually scares the kiddies, Moran had no time or inclination to shave, dutifully answering the call to meet Wiggles' managing director Mike Conway mid-morning on Tuesday.

Half an hour later he was allegedly terminated from his job as lead singer and offered a payout of about $60,000: a little more than four months of his reported $200,000-a-year wage.

Holly Byrnes, *The Daily Telegraph*, 20 January 2012

Sam Moran in the flesh appears a bigger, younger, hipper version of the safari-suited performer Aussie kids see each day on the Nick Jr channel. Six foot four if he's an inch, he stretches out on the couch and puts his hands behind his head, revealing a Michael Phelps-like wingspan. On the inside of his left arm is a loose cluster of small passport stamp tattoos, representing all the countries he's travelled to. It's Christmas Eve 2014 and Moran hates shaving, so a summertime beard has hatched again.

We are sitting in his office, which you enter through a dressmaker's shop on the third floor of a heritage building in one of Sydney's old dockside precincts. It has a casual student-like feel. There's a table football set up, a couple of old couches and a broken cello in the corner. High-end commercial real estate it is not, but the space does have a comfortable, creative atmosphere.

When we meet it is a month shy of three years since Moran was dumped from The Wiggles. I'm surprised he agreed to talk to me. Another Wiggles insider I'd arranged to interview pulled out at the last minute after checking with Paul Field. She wrote to me in an email: 'My confidentiality obligations to the company survive my employment with them and whilst there is nothing that I am hiding, from a legal perspective, it would be unwise for me to discuss this matter at any level.'

I had tried The Wiggles themselves through official channels, including our shared publisher, HarperCollins, and on Twitter and LinkedIn. I had emailed Wiggles ex-general manager Mike Conway several times and connected with him on LinkedIn but never received a response. I even posted a letter to Paul Field. A letter – with a stamp on it. In desperation, I approached Murray Cook at a pub in Sydney's inner west one night. We know people in common who rate him a top bloke. 'It wasn't our finest moment,' Cook said of Moran's departure, before politely moving away.

So it was with low expectations that I opened an SMS reply from Moran to my request for an interview. 'It is possible,' he wrote. Suddenly the drawbridge to Fortress Wiggles was down.

I relay my encounter with Cook to Moran and he looks up at the ceiling. Cook was the Wiggle Moran says he felt closest to, but they have not seen each other since Cook's departure.

'I haven't heard from any of them,' Moran says, 'except Greg. He asked to meet up. I think mainly because he was searching for answers. I think we were both sold different explanations. I think he felt portrayed as the villain … one of the villains.' (Page would later tell me that he had felt this way.)

Moran's life was twice upended by The Wiggles. First, when he was chosen to be the new Yellow Wiggle after serving as an understudy, backup singer and host of the *Dorothy the Dinosaur* show on and off for eight years. It was the mid-2000s. Moran and new wife Lyn – an American who played the part of Dorothy the Dinosaur during that period – were all set to move to the US to try their luck as 'struggling actors'. Then suddenly Moran was tapped to replace Page, who was suffering from a mystery illness. Moran and Lyn were so close to leaving for a new life in New York City that their wedding gift registry was set up in the US.

Moran recalls telling his flatmate, a Wiggles dancer, he had reached the end of the line with the children's troupe.

'I felt like I'd kind of done everything I could,' Moran says. 'I'd done recording, I'd done filming, I'd done all of these lives shows, and I'd filled in as a Wiggle.'

'It's not like I was ever going to *be* a Wiggle.'

Not long after that conversation, Page collapsed into Moran's arms at a meet-and-greet with families in Rhode Island, USA. Page – who was later diagnosed with orthostatic intolerance, a circulatory condition causing fainting – recounts the critical moment in his book, *Now and Then*: 'So there I was kneeling and talking to a child and when I stood up it felt like someone had literally drained the blood right out of me … I can recall Sam walking towards me and saying, "Do you feel OK?" I said, "No" … that's the last thing I remember.'

Less than a week later, Page left the group and Moran was the new Yellow Wiggle.

During the next five years, The Wiggles continued their conquest of America's kids and Australia's rich lists. In Moran's first year as a full-time Wiggle, the group generated $50 million in earnings, keeping them on top of *BRW* (*Business Review Weekly*) magazine's Entertainers Rich List, leaving Russell Crowe and AC/DC eating their dust. They were number one the next year too, earning $45 million and pipping Kylie Minogue. Things fell away a bit after the global financial crisis but they remained in *BRW*'s top five throughout, earning $28 million in Moran's final year as The Wiggles' front man. During this period, it was reported Moran had been negotiating a new contract, seeking a better cut of the action.

Then, even more suddenly than it started, life as a Wiggle was over – snuffed out in a morning meeting with Mike Conway. It emerged that a deal had been done in the background with a rejuvenated Page.

The Wiggles announced the switch straightaway, unleashing a torrent of emotion from invested parents.

'OMG OMG! Sad to see Sam go, but happy for Greg. Sounds stupid but I am in tears! Thank you Sam for all the love and awesomeness you have brought to the group' – Amanda Katherine Porter.

'Great that Greg is able to come back, but noooooooo, Sam is my favourite!' – Rhonda Bowman.

'Sam is the best thing that's happened to The Wiggles :(my girls will be devastated!' – Gaylene Matthewson.

'I'm happy Greg is well but my son loves Sam :(he's going to be very confused … Thanks for doing a fantastic job Sam xoxoxo' – Kimberley Menz.

Moran says the depth of feeling on Facebook surprised everyone. Until this point, he had been 'living in the bubble' of Wiggles world, a relentless touring environment lived on stage and in a tour bus. The band would arrive at a venue about 9am, and play a matinee show and then an evening spot at 6pm. It would be curtains by 9pm and onto the tour bus for a five-hour drive and 2am check-in at the next hotel. Then hit repeat. And repeat again.

Home was accessible only by internet and occasional phone calls in the early hours. Meanwhile, children around the world were sitting in front of the TV consuming The Wiggles day in, day out, forming a one-way friendship with the band.

When the personnel on the other side of that friendship was switched, the reaction from parents was overwhelming.

'It has always been a focus of The Wiggles to understand the part you play in the child's life for the day. But it might have been underestimated how much it plays a part in the parents' life on that day-to-day level as well,' Moran says.

'I know as a parent myself now, too, when your child gets lost in this fantasy world that they love, you get caught up in that fantasy a bit yourself. If you feel like your child's fantasy has been burst somehow then you feel like they've burst your fantasy too.'

Moran had first come into the orbit of The Wiggles' world aged 19 when he worked on a musical with John Field, who introduced him to the band. Aged 33 when he was shuttled off their planet, the only other job he'd ever held was as an IT salesman.

Once again Moran's life had been changed irrevocably by The Wiggles, but he says the fans' reaction gave him strength and direction at a time of crisis.

'I was surprised at the outpouring of support for me, which really encouraged me to just go down the path that I am now and continue to do what I was doing,' Moran says. 'Obviously people really loved what I do.'

Which prompts the question: why was Moran dumped and Page reinstated? Different reasons have been offered. In the *Today* interview, Field seemed to say he preferred Page's 'energy': 'I think it's more about the energy of The Wiggles … It wasn't so hard for me because the energy … I was feeling more like "Let's go down the Greg path" … The energy felt right.'

Journalists and fans speculated that Page was being offered a financial life raft by his old friends and business partners after reportedly losing a chunk of his Wiggles payout on realestate deals that turned turtle the GFC. Page denied this. 'Entirely false,' he said in the *Today* interview.

Paul Field told *The Sydney Morning Herald* the decision was made 'instinctively' after The Wiggles ran into Page at an ARIA Hall of Fame induction and realised he was 'full of beans'.

'Sam did an amazing job as his understudy and replacing [Page] for five years,' Field said. 'Clearly, you wouldn't be happy losing one of the best gigs on the planet. I understand that. But he also understands that the original singer is now able to come back.

'We are not a corporate get-together. We're a real group of mates.'

When I ask Moran how he felt after this key moment in Wiggles history, he says he was floored.

'You can only just shake your head at it,' he says. 'It's one of those things nobody seemed to understand at the time, like the parents. And I'd gotten no more understanding than anybody else, really, of why certain decisions were made and the way things were done.'

Moran says he gained clarity with the benefit of time and a later YouTube viewing of the *Today* interview. He chooses his words carefully around this subject.

MORAN: I had a few friends that said, 'You should watch it.'

ME: Yeah.

MORAN: I watched it, and at that time, because it was so soon, I didn't see what everybody else saw.

ME: Right.

MORAN: It was a very accurate picture of what I saw every day. So it wasn't until I got told to watch it again a few months later that I'd had enough space from it that I kind of saw what everybody else saw.

ME: What was that?

MORAN: [after pausing for five seconds] I guess it's more that I just understood the perspective that other people hadn't seen and that now they'd seen. It was a bit like the bubble had burst, I guess.

ME: What they were saying was that you'd been treated badly and that Anthony didn't like you.

MORAN: Right.

ME: Is that what you think that other people had seen?

MORAN: Yeah. More or less ...

Exit Cook, Fatt and Page

Accounts differ about the sequence of events leading up to the announcement that Cook, Page and Fatt were all leaving the group. It appears Fatt and Cook decided to throw in the towel about the same time – Fatt for health reasons (he'd had a pacemaker installed in 2011), and Cook because he wanted to spend more time with his family. Page's reasons for retirement were more mysterious. Why go through all that rejoining trauma only to leave again? It was a mystery he would explain later when we met.

Of course, these retirements had to happen at some stage, but the timing seemed strange. Many fans did not understand why Moran was not reinstated if youth was the issue.

Moran himself has a theory on the timing of the retirements. '[The Wiggles] were very aware that there is a three-year cycle in audience with preschool,' he says. 'Every three years we've got an entirely new audience that have never heard of you before, and parents too that have just become parents for the first time. So my speculation would be that [The Wiggles] had [taken] a very big hit and decided, if they were going to make a change at any point, they needed to do it all at once and just weather the storm.'

Moran says 'I'm just speculating' several times throughout our interview but his is not a bad theory. If I had to speculate myself, my version would go something like this:

Moran was different from the other Wiggles. Different in obvious ways, such as being 15 years younger and not being a part-owner of the operation. The fact remains that Moran's three band mates were also his employers.

There were also more subtle forces at play. Moran's background was in musical theatre. The others had deep roots in rock'n'roll. 'He's a smart guy but … it's different at sound checks,' Murray Cook told *San Diego CityBeat* in 2008. 'We kind of jam on things at those and he often doesn't know the songs we know. But we're slowly educating each other.' The original Wiggles had been in bands inspired by the sounds of the 1950s and 1960s. Chuck Berry, The Beatles and The Beach Boys were second nature. In the same newspaper interview, Cook mentioned the original Wiggles' shared background in early childhood education. They were old mates from university days – when Moran was still in primary school.

Perhaps it was more personal. The Wiggles were Anthony Field's band. Field was the creative spark at its inception. Field was the innovator. It was Field who fought his brothers' scepticism when he wanted to focus on kids' music while they were still part of the adult rock scene. He is The Wiggles' main man, the band leader. And it would appear Field developed some kind of issue with Moran.

He might have thought the young singer was getting too big for his boots. *The Sydney Morning Herald* reported that in the lead-up to Moran's departure, Field had not spoken off stage to his counterpart in Yellow for two years. In the same article, Paul Field defended his brother as a 'private person' who did not speak to anyone on tour, unless there was business to deal with. 'His time off between shows is mainly spent working out by himself and not socialising,' he said.

But if it were just a personal problem, there is no reason why the show could not have gone on. Look at Mick Jagger and Keith Richards, Paul McCartney and John Lennon, and everyone in Fleetwood Mac. Personal tension, even jealousy, can spur a band to great heights.

I think the bigger issue was that Moran was becoming a business problem. The more entrenched Moran became, the more his value rose. This could cause issues down the line, complicating succession planning. One of the first lessons of business is: do not dilute your equity. It is obvious why the other Wiggles would have opposed handing over a percentage of the franchise to anyone, not just Moran. He did not build the business from scratch. Why cut him in?

Then why not just pay him more – say, double his salary? For the simple reason that this would affect profitability. It could also set the pay rate for the next generation of salaried Wiggles. If everyone is doing much the same job, everyone should be paid the same. How could management justify having Moran on $300,000 per year and any newcomers on $150,000? When Cook and Fatt and eventually Field retired, Moran would be the dominant public face of The Wiggles. He would have the bargaining power of a world-class soccer striker in future salary negotiations.

I would speculate that all this had been worked through by the Field brothers and Mike Conway. All the pieces were in place and they were coloured Yellow, Blue, Red and Purple. For The Wiggles to flourish from that point, the uniforms would need to outlive the performers.

When Page was reinstated – as a salaried member, not as the partner he once was – The Wiggles got a taste of just how popular Moran had become. More than a taste: the backlash took some real momentum out of the business. Financial year 2013 was their worst for earnings in a decade, according to *BRW*.

However, it was evident The Wiggles needed to move to the new model at some stage in the following five or so years. Whether or not the timing was coincidental, the decisions of Page, Cook and Fatt to retire meant, as Moran suggested, The Wiggles took their second big hit in that same generation of preschoolers (and parents). This made business sense even if it appeared nonsensical in other ways.

Consider the ruthlessness of the nappy industry – the fierce competition for dollars in a perennial market where the consumer cycle is even more compressed than the three-year horizon Moran mentioned. Children are only in nappies for an average of 24 months but there are new customers born every minute. From the inception of this book, we have called this chapter 'The Hard Men of The Wiggles'. It is a nice 'reverse', as we term it in Share Wars (see Chapter 7): an idea that is compelling because it is contradictory at its core. It is playing on the same irony as the nappy industry, that small people's business is big business, and that ruthlessness can lurk behind cuteness.

The Wiggles have refused to talk to me. The only impression I can gain of them is through their books and news quotes, and through other people. Moran calls Paul the heart of The Wiggles and Anthony the brains. Some say Anthony's ability to connect with children approaches genius. Together they have built something extraordinary that has brightened the lives of millions around the world, including many very ill children. In his own words, Anthony reveals himself as a reclusive, sensitive performer who has suffered chronic pain and addiction. He appears to be a difficult man but not a hard man. He is the band leader, but the decision not to renew Moran's contract is one The Wiggles must own as a group. It was a tough call but the show has gone on.

Just before this book went to press, Paul Field made contact. He wrote in an email that he did not want to speak to me in case it reignited the controversy of three years ago. He also said the Wiggles organisation had made it clear it did not want to comment.

This was an understandable position but it showed that Field thought, or at least hoped, The Wiggles could control their story; that it was proprietary and somehow invalid without their authorisation. But in the end another former Wiggle *did* talk to me, revealing a fascinating alternate version of the events that unfolded three years ago. I made contact with Greg Page through our mutual publisher, HarperCollins. The original Yellow Wiggle was keen to get his side of the story across but suspected I was unsympathetic.

Greg Page arrives at our meeting with some bits of paper and a game plan. His strategy seems to be threefold: gauge my sympathies; convince me he only returned to The Wiggles because he was told Moran was leaving; and compel me to consider speculation that Moran wasn't dumped but actually wanted to leave the band. I tell Page that nothing I have seen or read – including quotes from Paul Field – indicated Moran was happy about losing the Yellow skivvy.

Page hands me a draft press release from the time, which he had approved but was never sent: '[Page] returns in an interim role until a permanent replacement is found for Sam Moran, who has left The Wiggles to pursue other interests.'

An interim role. That's a game changer. Page's agreeing upfront to a short-term stint in Yellow would explain why he retired again so soon after rejoining the band.

Even more stunning is Page's assertion that he was sounded out by Conway way back in September 2011. He says Conway told him then that Moran was leaving The Wiggles. This was a good four months before Moran – or anyone else – found out he was toast.

'I was asked to come back because, to quote the business manager at the time, "Sam is unhappy and will be leaving at the end of the year",' Page said. 'That's the only basis that I agreed to return upon – the fact that Sam was leaving.'

If Moran was departing, Page was filling an existing vacancy. If the public had known Page only joined as a stop-gap measure and that this followed Moran's decision to depart on his own terms, there would have been very little backlash at all. Facebook would not have melted down. Lorraine Speirs in the UK would have got some sleep. Shattered Ashlee Newton would still be intact. Parents would not have had to choose sides. There would have been no Teaming.

But history records a different reality, and the social tremor around the retirement story was detected, captured and filed by the Likeable Engine in May 2012, a digital artefact alongside millions of others in our database.

I can understand why Page sought out Moran afterwards. Although Anthony Field was cast as the villain in news and social media, Page suffered collateral damage. Many were unkind in their assessment of the original Yellow's motivations and financial position. It seems likely Page thought he was helping The Wiggles out before they transitioned to the next Yellow Wiggle. Remember Moran's description of their discussion after the fact? Page thinks they were sold different lines. I think he's right. Both men were played like vintage Telecasters.

I went back to Moran for his recollections of his final months in The Wiggles, to check whether it was his choice to leave: the theory Page had urged me to consider. Moran said it was not.

'I had been attempting to initiate a promised employment review at a previously agreed date and was stonewalled for six months,' he wrote by email. 'No discussion constituting an employment review or terms ever managed to take place.'

This story has serious implications for the reputations and careers of the main players. It is an episode Page refers to as a 'huge mess ... still', and a period that weighs particularly heavily on both ex-Yellows.

Part of the reason for this is that the emotions of parents were amplified and sustained through Facebook, and that this shaped mainstream media coverage. Seven or eight years ago, the outrage would have been limited to a few vox pops on the evening news and some letters to the editor. But the intervening growth of Facebook meant Wiggles fans were mobilised the moment Moran was de-skivvied. Likers and haters – and all those in between – now had a broadcast platform. No one was holding back. And although Moran and Page were criticised by some fans, it was Field who copped the brunt.

As mentioned, few subjects fire up Facebook more than children and their welfare. Children are incendiary. Witness the approval of the father who killed his child's abuser, a story at the extreme end of a highly charged continuum. The Wiggles' tale is at the other end, different in every way except for one. The message Sharingland sent was loud and clear: do not mess with the kids, or you will face the wrath of their parents.

The saga also highlights Teaming behaviour. People were using this story to broadcast their point of view. Team Sam or Team Greg? Are you for Anthony or against him? This was sharing that had nothing to do with people serving their networks. This was sharing by people taking a stand. Not all your friends Like this. They are choosing sides. They want you to choose sides too.

Chapter 7

The Reverse

By Hal Crawford

Bundaberg, 1935: a town of hard-drinking larrikins. Cane-cutters and cattlemen, and plenty of unemployed drifting up from the south looking for work. These are hard years: the deep Depression. Everyone needs a laugh, a drink, preferably both, and preferably before lunchtime.

The pub is crowded. Beer and rum on the counters waiting for their owners to finish the drinks in their hands. A dog walks in. It's no one's dog, a stray, with nothing in its stomach and a vague idea that that could change. No worse off than half the men in there – one more mongrel. But the dog is not bright. Gets caught up in the forest of legs, causes a man to stumble. The man kicks the dog. The terrified animal vaults onto the counter, sending glass and booze everywhere as it skitters about, evading capture. The caper ends when the dog runs straight into the big arms of a cane-man, who cradles it like a baby. The drinkers cheer.

The man straightens the dog's ear, raises the animal and opens his own mouth. The bar is quiet the moment before the farmer's teeth come down. He bites the dog's ear, hard. The dog yelps, wriggles and is off like a rocket, into the dirt street and daylight. The entire pub erupts and every man there knows he has a story to tell later, in other places. The farmer is handed a bottle of rum. Drinks are on the house.

The essence of a good story

What makes a good news story? A tough question to answer. There are so many things – so many diverse areas that are of interest to different audiences, so much that changes over time – that isolating a single factor inherent to the news itself is not possible. News is not like that. For editors or theorists working in the old data-poor world of traditional news there was one example, though, that was relied on more than any other to convey the essence of a good story: 'Man bites dog.'

The tale is still dusted off as an example of good news by crusty editors who are only being half-ironic; it has served as a kind of instructional joke for more than a century. While 'Dog bites man' is a poor story, 'Man bites dog' is a cracking yarn. The power of the story is usually explained in terms of the likeliness of the occurrences – how common it is for a dog to bite and how rare for a man – but there's more at play here than that.

'Man bites dog' is a 'reverse': a story where the opposite of the expected happens. It's not just about noting a small discrepancy, refining your world view with a piece of new information. It's a contradiction of what is expected anywhere in the patterns of life – work, health, love, war, family. Not only is it uncommon for a man to bite a dog, the event represents an entire reversal of roles where the human descends to the level of the brute.

This story structure, held out as an example in the days of hot-lead presses, still works in the world of social media. Within the top lists of shared stories in any period there are always a number of reverses, so much so that the genre deserves special mention. For example, our Likeable Engine data shows that four of the top 50 shared Australian news stories in 2014 were reverses. The top three of these were:

- 'World laughs with praising tradies': video of workmen yelling out compliments to passing women (part of a viral ad campaign)
- 'Young Hockey protests against uni fees in video': the young Joe Hockey, who as Australian Treasurer wants to deregulate university fees entirely, campaigns as a student against university fees
- 'Snake eats crocodile after epic fight'

The fourth story I'd like to dwell on a bit longer. Like the other three, it centres on a video, but unlike the other three it is not Australian. From the city of Bakersfield in California, the footage is somewhat compressed vertically, so the trees look shorter, the cars squatter and the people stockier than in real life. The video has a time stamp counting out the seconds from 4:50:48pm at the centre top of the frame.

CAMERA 1:

A curved suburban street. In the middle distance, a white SUV parked in a driveway and a little boy playing on a bike. There's a palm tree in the middle of the frame.

The bike is a balance bike, too small for the boy. His knees are bent nearly at right angles as he trundles along the footpath then up the driveway next to the family car.

CAMERA 2:

In the foreground, a wooden picket fence.

A dog wanders out from behind the fence, sniffing the air. This dog is muscular but not huge. He spots something to the left of camera, his body tenses and he's off after it.

CAMERA 3:

Another camera, this on the other side of the family SUV we saw before. The dog progresses quickly from right to left, moving behind the back tyre of the SUV.

CAMERA 1:

Back on the other side of the vehicle, the boy is standing up, looking off camera towards his house. The dog rounds the back of the SUV and approaches carefully from behind him, inspecting the boy's body. He settles on the left leg. With great force the dog bites the child, dragging him to the ground then backwards, shaking him from side to side.

A cat emerges from the direction of the house. It is running as fast as a cat can run, hurtling directly into the dog. In the last moment before impact the cat turns its head and lets its body slam into the dog. This cat-projectile knocks the dog away from the boy.

The dog releases its grip on the boy's leg and runs in a wide arc back around the SUV, off camera. The cat follows. As the animal chase starts, a woman appears and runs to the boy, whose prone body is now obscured by the palm tree. She's barefoot, wearing a pink dress of thin fabric. She squats by the boy.

CAMERA 3:

The cat chases the dog up the street. After a few metres the cat stops with a flourish, tail in the air, and returns the way it came. The dog runs off screen right.

CAMERA 1:

The woman in the pink dress stands and runs away from the boy. She runs wide-legged, bent-kneed, with her hands out, disappearing off screen top right. The boy stands, leaving his bike on the ground, and runs wide-legged, bent-kneed, with his hands out, to the front of the SUV. The cat returns to the boy.

The cat's owner and husband of the woman in the pink dress, Roger Triantafilo, published the video on YouTube under the title 'My cat saved my son' at 5am on 14 May, nine days after the attack. Within three hours he was being contacted by US national media.

Triantafilo, a database administrator, is keen on security. He runs an eight-camera CCTV system outside his house that captures every second of footage to disk. He also happens to be surrounded by friends who are media professionals. One, Ron Hashim, became his media advisor, while another, Crosby Shaterian, worked for 23ABC News in social media. Hashim had taken out ownership of the site address taratheherocat. com and Facebook and Twitter accounts pre-emptively before Triantafilo decided to embrace viral stardom.

'It was really daunting at first because you just get so many requests and you're just hammered with all of this media interest around the story,' Triantafilo said. 'My buddy, Crosby, asked me if I wanted to go on the news here and talk about it and I told him, "No I don't really care to."'

That changed after his wife agreed to an interview, and for the next three days the Triantafilos had a tight schedule.

'I don't think people realise how much work goes on behind the scenes with something like this,' says Triantafilo. 'Doing interviews, managing a website, managing Facebook and all the socials and then pushing that across Twitter and Instagram.'

Being in the eye of the viral storm was not pleasant, particularly when the comments turned nasty – offering what Triantafilo calls 'negative support', more commonly known as 'criticism' – around aspects of the video that didn't meet their approval.

'People were saying, "I'm glad your son got bit" and "Why did your wife run away?"'

Triantafilo is downplaying the vile insults directed at his wife. The 'negative supporters' fixated on the way his wife ran off screen rather than staying with her injured son. The criticism didn't make sense – she was going after the dog to neutralise the threat – but Triantafilo got on the comments stream and answered anyway.

After three days Triantafilo was contacted by Jukin Media, a company that makes money for amateurs who find themselves with a viral video hit on their hands. As a result, Triantafilo says, he has licensed the video to 'some media outlets' and has been paid for appearances but 'we really haven't made a lot of money in this phase'. He has given some of the cash to animal charity SPCA. This move – defusing criticisms of cynical money-making – gives the impression of coming out of a marketing playbook.

As with 'Grumpy Cat', an animal famed for its underbite, Triantafilo and Hashim were trying to create a star. Before the initial wave of enthusiasm for the video had subsided, Hashim created a TARA HEROCAT logo featuring what looks like a crescent moon, three paws and a stylised cat's head. You can buy this logo as a car sticker, or printed on three different kinds of T-shirt. At the bottom of the official site, headlined 'Discover #HEROCAT', is the phrase 'Now the world knows'.

In one of the cat's numerous television appearances immediately after the attack, TMZ executive producer Harvey Levin nailed why anybody cared in the first place: 'You do realise that your cat has probably changed America's view, maybe the whole of the world's view, on cats more than any other animal in the history of cats?'

What 'the world now knows' is that its generic view of cats as self-centred non team players has been upset by irrefutable video proof of ferocious feline loyalty. Where dogs are famed for both faithfulness and cat-baiting, here the tables were perfectly turned.

The sites, the Facebook page, the Twitter account, appearances on national television: the Triantafilos and their advisors went in hard. But what, really, was there to talk about? The story was contained in 40 seconds of video. It was over with the pictures of 10 stitches in a little boy's leg and the news that Scrappy the dog had been put down.

Survival of the fittingest

The reverse is one of the many story types that survived from old world to new. The cat story earned tens of thousands of Likes and Tara's Facebook account still has 47,000 fans. The fact that the reverse pre-dates newspapers by at least a couple of thousand years indicates it will also be around after Zuckerberg's empire has crumbled.

Take the parable of the Good Samaritan in the Bible. Its power derives from a straight-up reverse. A man, probably a Jew, is beaten up and left for dead on the side of the road. His plight is ignored by a priest and another Jewish man. A third man wanders by and, seeing this awful mess of a person, comes to his aid. He cleans the victim's wounds, puts him on his donkey and takes him to an inn, where he pays for his recuperation. The odd thing is, the third man is a Samaritan, and Samaritans and Jews have been expressly forbidden by their leaders to even talk to each other. Violence between the two groups is common. A Palestinian paying for the hospital care of a Jewish settler in present-day Israel would be less surprising. That's why Jesus pulled the story out when he wanted to make a point that would be remembered. Really love your neighbour, okay?

Shakespeare also loves a reverse, with one of his characters, Prince Hal, appreciating how the turning of tables will create a story with a long shelf-life: 'Now could thou and I rob the thieves and go merrily to London, it would be argument for a week, laughter for a month, and a good jest forever.'

Once you are aware of the reverse as an idea, you start to see it everywhere. Beethoven, the model of a musical genius, was deaf. He crafted his most sublime music while his world grew more and more silent. Beethoven started going deaf in his thirties, becoming isolated by his inability to hear conversation. By the time he wrote and conducted his final symphony, the epic Ninth, he was so profoundly deaf he had to be turned around to know that the audience was rapturously applauding.

We've established that this principle of contradicting expectations works well in getting people's attention, and in holding it. The question is why.

Hegel in reverse

The German philosopher Wilhelm Hegel was an extraordinary guy. Apparently his lectures were so excruciatingly boring that to sit through one while he hemmed and hawed in a monotone of unintelligible philosophical babble was regarded as an achievement worth telling people about. Those early self-proclaimed 'Hegelians' were a rare band. The students first had to apply themselves to the difficult task of working out what Hegel was actually saying, then remember the philosophical background to make sense of the point, and then guess how to apply it in the real world. *Herr Doktor* was not generous with examples. He preferred the abstract to the particular. To top it off, the students were paying this teacher by the lecture, in cash. Either in spite of Hegel's mind-numbing style or because of it, some found intense reward in what the man was saying.

Hegel was born in the same year as Beethoven, 1770.

You and I won't ever know just what that time was like, but it must have been quite a ride. Within a lifetime the world would go from a place ruled by kings and ancient traditions to one in the thrall of freedom, technology and the power of reason. Everything was in violent upheaval in a period when the French Revolution had, in a stroke, not just broken with the past, but destroyed it. This upheaval was felt strongly in the lands the French ruler Napoleon Bonaparte was conquering.

In 1806, that included the part of Germany where Hegel was living, in the town of Jena.

On 13 October of that year Hegel was walking the streets. He had a number of things on his mind, and 'the Old Man', as the philosopher had been known since his undergraduate days, was more bent and ponderous than ever.

Take, for example, his academic career. It was going nowhere. Worse men than him were getting well-paid positions at prestigious universities, while he was slowly fading into obscurity. A fellow he despised, Jakob Fries, had just been promoted. The injustice of it twisted around in Hegel's mind. This was he who had plumbed the depths of the processes that drove the world. He who at that moment was holding a bundle of paper that was literally the culmination of all thinking to that point in history. Nothing less. What did Fries have that Hegel did not? The answer was clear. Fries had a book.

Hegel needed to publish. He had been promising 'my book' to everyone for years. The phrase now rang hollow: 'When my book is finished.' Many mornings he had sat at the miserable table in his miserable lodgings and wondered whether his book – the high point of Western culture – would ever see the light of day.

All the procrastination and broken promises had led to this moment. In five days' time his manuscript was due in Bamberg, and he would make sure it arrived. It was his friend Niethammer who had first arranged for the prestigious Goebhardt to print 1000 copies of the book. His genius had been quantified at 18 florins per page. The deal had been done; he had been promised he would get half the money when he had delivered half the book. But of course that never happened. Half a book does not exist. These things are birthed whole or not at all. A year after Hegel missed the first deadline, Goebhardt had turned nasty, and it was only when Niethammer intervened and guaranteed that he would pay should the philosopher screw up again that the printer relented. That new deadline was 18 October.

Hegel had reached the town square, surprised for a moment to find it virtually empty, until he saw a small group of soldiers on the other side. They wore white trousers and blue jackets. French. The war. With all the thought of Goebhardt and Niethammer and that cretin Fries it had slipped his mind. How would the manuscript get through with war in the vicinity and the town already occupied?

A fresh wave of anxiety swamped Hegel as he watched the soldiers march off through the mist. Now he smelled the gunpowder on the air. He shifted the manuscript he had been carefully holding under his arm. Everything was riding on this manuscript. No book, no money, no career.

He continued walking, and when he reached the staging inn, entrusted the package to the postmaster. 'This contains my System,' he told the man. 'It's the only copy.'

The war was on and the manuscript must get out. He would not disappoint Niethammer again. He began the trek back to the other side of the river, where he was staying for the duration of the emergency, thanking God he didn't have to return to his own house and his landlady Mrs Burkhardt. Dear Mrs Burkhardt, with her open heart. What she gave so freely came at a heavy cost. He couldn't doubt her sincerity. She was pregnant. The child was his. What would happen to her and the baby?

So it was that, thinking of his landlady, Hegel encountered Napoleon.

Jena is surrounded by hills, and the town itself slopes up towards the north. As he traversed one of the major roads leading in that direction, Hegel had a view of where the old town wall ended, a few hundred metres distant. A column of French cavalry were riding out into the open land. What he saw in an instant was a commotion that had been hidden by the buildings of the occupied town. Behind the cavalry was a small group of mounted officers, and there at the head, not 200 metres from where he stood, was the Emperor Napoleon. The man was conspicuous in his plain hat and coat among the gaudy cavalry officers.

Writing to Niethammer later about the experience, Hegel said this: 'I saw the Emperor – this world-soul – riding out of the city on reconnaissance. It is indeed a wonderful sensation to see such an individual, who, concentrated here at a single point, astride a horse, reaches out over the world and masters it.'

All Hegel's anxiety disappeared. Napoleon was the living demonstration of Hegel's system of thought. The man who had conquered the world was just a year older than he. When Hegel returned to his temporary lodgings, safe in the knowledge he was under the same roof as several French officers, he began work on the preface to the manuscript he had entrusted to the post that day. He wrote: 'It is not difficult to see that ours is a birth-time and a period of transition to a new era … The gradual crumbling behind the scenes that left the face of things unaltered is cut short by a sunburst which in a flash illuminates the new world.'

He was not only talking about Napoleon. He was also referring to himself and his System. In Hegel's letters and papers we get a clear sense of a man aware of his own participation in a historical process. It is invigorating not just to recognise in Hegel but to apply it to yourself. We are all players. It helps explain why students sat through Hegel's lectures, and why 'the Old Man' maintains a following to this day.

The next morning just after dawn the Prussian and French armies clashed in a monumental battle on a plateau north of Jena. Thousands of men died, killed by rifle shot, cannon and bayonet in an engagement that once again demonstrated Napoleon's martial genius. The Prussians were hopeless, and hopelessly routed, fleeing the battlefield in the tens of thousands. Their antiquated command and communications structures had left them in the wrong places, in the wrong numbers, with the wrong orders. Every moment of every day since the war's conception almost a year earlier – in a secret midnight meeting between the Prussian king and queen and the Russian tsar – had revealed the shortcomings of the old order.

By 3pm it was all over. In a day's bloody work, the French had demonstrated a superiority in arms that stemmed directly from a superiority in ideology. Everything about Napoleon's Grande Armée was more efficient. This was Reason putting Tradition to the sword.

Contradiction makes the world go round

Let me fly back to Prince Hal for a moment. Shakespeare's character begins a lout and ends a king, and a good one. Among Hal's many observations about the world is his comment that 'If all the year were playing holidays, To sport would be as tedious as to work.'

Hegel took that requirement for differentiation, for variation from the norm, and upped the stakes. In his philosophical meanderings he used a 'dialectic' technique that he believed was uniquely suited to the job of understanding the world, because the world actually progressed through a dialectic process. The basis of the method is to take something seemingly stable – the monarchies of Europe, for example – and to observe the flaws and contradictions within it that give rise to an antagonist – the French Revolution, for example. The antagonist, the French Revolution, being defined in opposition, is too unbalanced to exist on its own and in turn gives way to something combining elements of monarchy and revolution. In this instance, Hegel was convinced history had come to a stable conclusion with the modern Prussian state following the battle of Jena.

The existence of conflict is a crucial element in Hegel's dialectical scheme. Without an internally generated contradiction, no movement is possible in the world. Existence itself is out of the question.

The light needs the dark. The monarchy needs the revolution. As much as he despises him, Hegel needs his nemesis Jakob Fries. We understand only in the presence of contradiction, and through this understanding the world moves forward.

The manuscript made it through the French lines and the chaos of panicked Prussians to Bamberg. It became Hegel's first book, *The Phenomenology of Mind*. At first it received horrible reviews. Hegel's kind of philosophy was old-fashioned, and some people, including Fries, thought he was a fraud – an unsalaried lecturer with ambition that outrode his ability. Hegel's financial and emotional pain in Jena became more acute, to the point where he was begging everyone he knew for a job. He tried to convince one of his better placed friends, the brilliant Johann Wolfgang von Goethe, to make him professor of botany. He knew nothing about plants, but who cares when you have described the whole shebang? Mere detail was the elaboration of a general process. As he pointed out to a friend in a letter, somewhat mystified by his own abstract tendencies: 'I do not know why I always fall into general reflections.' Goethe wasn't convinced and Hegel didn't get the job.

The friend who came through was Niethammer. This true believer, who had already staked money and reputation on the philosopher, found Hegel a well-paid position in Bamberg. Despite not having two florins to rub together, Hegel was wary of the job and tried to find a way out. Eventually, after Goethe had turned him down and other opportunities had fallen through, he accepted and prepared to move. The future author of the weighty ethical treatise *The Philosophy of Right* left behind Mrs Burkhardt and her newly born baby, putting a couple of hundred kilometres between himself and his illegitimate son. Ludwig, named after Hegel's brother, would end up in an orphanage. It was not until Hegel was married with other children that he accepted Ludwig into his household. The boy died in battle at 24, a victim of one of those 'movements of the world spirit' his father loved to understand.

The crowning reverse in Hegel's life of contradictions has to be the Bamberg job. The man whose writing 'is almost uniquely obscure [and] positively repels the reader' was going to become a newspaper editor.

Opposites attract meaning

Reverses are everywhere, and the reason they are everywhere is that they fit the way we understand the world. Hegel would say they *are* the way we understand the world. To better comprehend the concept of a child, let's take the reverse of a child – a child who does the opposite of what a child is supposed to do. For example: Aldi Rizal lives in a village in Sumatra. He was found by an enterprising reporter with a video camera who got word of the village's 'smoking baby'. What the reporter's footage shows is a fat-cheeked toddler in a run-down yard, eyeballing the camera without a shred of concern. He lifts a cigarette to his mouth, inhales deeply, and exhales. Surrounded by smoke, Aldi is a self-aware and defiant presence. But he's sitting on a tricycle, wearing a nappy.

The smoking baby and his two-pack-a-day habit were discovered in 2010. The world found this reverse irresistible, even while condemning his parents. It turned out smoking babies were not so uncommon in Indonesia, and as the international reporting teams flew into Sumatra, more fuming children came out of the woodwork. They didn't rate: the value of the reverse had been exhausted.

Some instances are longer lived – for example, the reporting of scientific findings on coffee, chocolate and alcohol. These substances, generally regarded as indulgent if not actively bad for you, have been the subject of thousands of news items reporting research into their surprising health benefits. These reports keep hitting the same button – 'Six reasons why chocolate is actually GOOD for you' – despite the fact that the same point has been made several thousand times previously. No doubt the confectionary and beverage industries and our own appetites are partly responsible for the popularity of these pieces.

I could go on. The reverses of the generous pauper, the loyal prostitute, the ungodly priest all get our attention, whether in fiction or reporting. The contradiction helps define the original; opposition helps us understand the world.

The strength of a scientific model is not determined by its elegance or descriptive power alone. True scientific worth also requires the ability to predict accurately.

Hegel's intellectual descendants treated his dialectical theory of history as science and used it to make predictions. The most famous of these predictions, by a German exile living in London, observed that the capitalist economy had created a workforce alienated from the system, denied the fruits of its own labour. These workers were the structural contradiction that would oppose the owners of capital, leading to the birth of a new order. The new system was Communism and the man beavering away at it was Karl Marx. He believed his Communist state would happen come what might: it was the nature of capitalism to create the alienated workforce that would destroy it.

It didn't turn out that way. The brutality of capitalism's excesses was moderated and worldwide revolution thwarted. The capitalist strongholds of Britain and the US held firm. In the industrial nations the dialectic fizzed out like a bomber's dud. Elsewhere Marx's work was used to justify violence on a scale that would have horrified even that blood-thirsty 'world-soul' Napoleon.

Hegel can't be blamed for Marx. 'The Old Man' would not have approved of the revolutionary. He didn't believe for one moment that labour and capital were going to go to war; he thought history had come to its conclusion with the modern Prussian state. For Hegel, everything was settled. He had no idea that a teenager from Trier, who was just 13 the year Hegel died, would one day appropriate his dialectic. For his part, Marx had no idea that millions would be killed in the name of the ideology he had crafted. In real life, nothing is ever settled and no one knows what's going to happen next.

So Marx took Hegel and ran with him, sitting in the big new Reading Room in the courtyard of the British Museum. That magnificent example of 19th-century design, with so much unnecessary space above your head and a ceiling made from papier-mâché, was a welcome refuge for the German. Marx, like Hegel, was down on his luck and making do with what he could scrounge off a mate. In this case that mate was Friedrich Engels, a man as loyal as Niethammer, if not quite as well-connected. Marx was both revolutionary and patriarch, and had three children, a wife, a German cook and three dogs to support. He loved and enjoyed this household and had a jolly streak in him, as evidenced by the reminiscences of Marian Comyn, a friend of his daughter Eleanor:

> As an audience he was delightful, never criticising, always
> entering into the spirit of any fun that was going, laughing
> when anything struck him as particularly comic, until the
> tears ran down his cheeks – the oldest in years, but in spirit
> as young as any of us. And his friend, the faithful Frederic
> Engels, was equally spontaneous.
>
> **Marian Comyn, *My Recollections of Karl Marx***

But Marx was skint. In the end, just like Hegel, Marx had to turn to journalism to make ends meet: the co-author of *The Communist Manifesto* landed a gig with the *New-York Tribune*.

Marx covered world affairs, working from London to describe what was happening in Europe for an American audience. Among his hundreds of columns are pieces on the death penalty, the price of corn and the charge of the Light Brigade at Balaclava. The proponent of class struggle and world socialism was actually a pretty good correspondent. He was never reticent about sharing an opinion and he churned out the copy, working for 10 years under the direction of editor Charles A. Dana. The pair had made contact in France in the 'year of revolutions', 1848, when Dana was covering the European upheavals for the *Tribune*. Dana became a legend of the newspaper world, going on to found the New York *Sun*. He was one of the originals who created the model for the newspaper editor – fearless, fair and, above all, a master of story. He shared with his London correspondent a love of Shakespeare and a view that the playwright was 'indispensable to a journalist'. You may also be interested to learn that Dana is widely attributed as the original source of the 'Man bites dog' advice.

Despite this connection to Dana, his status as a dog owner and his documented love of fun, a review of Marx's decade of newspaper work sadly fails to turn up any animal reporting at all.

Hegel edited the *Bamberger Zeitung* for over a year. I would love to know whether during that period, 1807 to 1808, the paper its new editor had described as 'not quite respectable' found space between the pro-Napoleonic rants to publish any news about dogs.

I may seem preoccupied with dogs, but the data backs me up. Dogs are uniquely attractive to the news-reading public. Our 2012 survey of the Likeable data found dogs twice as likely as cats to feature in a highly shared story. Even more telling, dogs are twice as likely as cats to feature in *any* story, regardless of how much it is shared. A scan of headlines for the whole data set for our first three-month collection period – 1.4 million articles from 118 news sites – shows that dogs make more news than any other non-human animal. Cats do alright. But they do even better when a dog is involved. Just look at Tara (I'm not going to call her 'the hero cat').

The data could go some way to explain the endurance of 'Man bites dog'. Somehow the popularity of this animal sank into the press's institutional mind, bubbled around in there and then got spat out in this story. Here's the news item from 1935 that we began the chapter with:

THIS IS REAL NEWS
BUNDABERG FARMER BIT A DOG

BRISBANE, Monday. When a man's beer is upset he may be excused for taking drastic action. Possibly Lord Northcliffe's famous dictum, "When a man bites a dog it's news," may never have been heard by the farmer who gave Bundaberg real news, avenged his beer, and won for himself the esteem of his fellow townsmen.

The bar of a Bundaberg hotel was crowded with thirsty men when a stray dog entered. After becoming entangled in the feet of the patrons it sought refuge from kicks and curses on the bar counter.

Pots and noggins with their contents were scattered in all directions, and the unfortunate dog became Public Enemy No. 1.

A brawny cane farmer found a prompt and effective remedy when he gathered the dog in his arms and smartly and scientifically bit it on the ear.

With a yelp of surprise the disturber dashed for the door, and the biter was treated to drinks on the house.

The Newcastle Herald, Monday, 3 June 1935

There's one problem with the most famous reverse in all of journalism. Have another look at the article above. The biggest headline reads 'THIS IS REAL NEWS', and the lead paragraph quotes 'Lord Northcliffe's famous dictum'. Already we know the provenance of the story is under question. And shouldn't it be Dana's dictum? Ignore that for a moment. Without Northcliffe – the British magnate who began life as

Alfred Harmsworth and built a newspaper empire powerful enough to get him a new name – would we have a story? Would the news of a farmer biting a dog make it all the way from Bundaberg to Newcastle, 1000 kilometres away, if the attraction was actually in the event itself? Not in this case. It's printed here as a reference to an amusing definition of news, something that appealed to the people making the newspaper.

The same is true for every 'Man bites dog' item that appears in the historical record. The earliest reference in Australia occurs in 1906 with the reprinting of an item from the *New Orleans Times-Democrat*, attributing the 'Man bites dog' quote to an anonymous retired American newspaperman who was talking about what makes a good story. Lord Northcliffe is nowhere to be seen. That giant of newspaper history certainly used the dictum – he is reported in *The Sydney Morning Herald* as having defined news as 'Man bites dog' in a speech while visiting Australia in 1921 – but whether he appropriated with intent or was just winging it is unknown.

That the first Australian mention should refer to a US newspaperman points to the American origin of the saying, and this is backed up by more extensive research. The Quote Investigator site has checked out the history of the 'Man bites dog' story and come to the startling conclusion that the original source is an American work of fiction. The following line is delivered in an 1899 short story called 'The Old Reporter' by fictional journalist Billy Woods:

Now, for instance, 'A dog bites a man' – that's a story; 'A man bites a dog' – that's a good story.

Woods is the eponymous central character, a drunk perpetually ashamed he doesn't have a university degree. The man can nevertheless find and write a story better than anyone else at his newspaper. Playwright Jesse Lynch Williams wrote 'The Old Reporter' after working for several years at *The Sun* under none other than Charles A. Dana. Dana had moved on from wrangling his European correspondent Karl Marx to pioneering campaign journalism, taking a Democratic line that influenced the history of the nation.

So here we have more evidence that points towards Dana as the original source of 'Man bites dog'. Of course, it's possible Williams heard the story from one of the old hands at the paper, or invented it himself, as a kind of organic expression of newsroom wisdom. But it's also possible he heard it first from his editor and transferred it to the mouth of a fictional character.

'Man bites dog' is still trotted out from time to time as a news item: a 2012 version in *The Sydney Morning Herald* appeared under the headline 'Man bites dog. No, seriously'. Either explicitly or implicitly, it is 'meta', referencing the old reporter's advice. It is a story about a story. These stories are being published not for the news but for the headline: a light-hearted idea that ends in three paragraphs of lame copy. There's a reason for this. The crowning reverse of the archetypal reverse is that, actually, 'Man bites dog' is a terrible story. It got that way some time between when a fictional character gave fictional advice to a fictional cub reporter in 1899, and when a UK newspaper magnate delivered a stolen anecdote at a stuffy dinner 20 years later.

ALL YOUR FRIENDS LIKE THIS

Be alert and aware

The value in the simple concept of the reverse is in priming an editor or a reporter to recognise a great story in the wild. It's very difficult to reverse-engineer reverses out of whole cloth – I have tried – but it pays to be ready when the moment actually comes. For example, my advice to reporters would be that if they find any of the following:

- a surgeon on the dole
- an ebullient undertaker
- a fox that lives happily with chickens

they should publish the story immediately. It will do well on social networks. Bearing Hegel in mind, it is wise to draw out the contradictions in your subject matter. Find the cat – show how it overcomes the dog and defends a child. Find the moral philosopher – show him caving in to desire then abandoning his child. Find a story that is supposed to be the pinnacle of good news judgement – show how it is actually an in-joke that has left readers scratching their heads for a century.

Chapter 8

The Hoaxers

By Andrew Hunter

Anyone who holds the internet guilty of destroying journalism should read the *Spokane Falls Chronicle* of 14 October 1890. The cracks were showing back then despite the proliferation of dead trees. Advertisements are presented as editorial. A story about people marrying corpses in China sits above an item recommending Electric Bitters for readers suffering 'nervous prostration'. You are likely afflicted if you cannot eat, think, sleep or 'do anything to your satisfaction'. This is not marked as advertising.

The edition also shows how journalistic storytelling has evolved. We read about a rich young man who 'blew his brains out' in a gentleman's club in New York after a week of insomnia and – as one friend puts it – a lifetime of hypochondria. God knows how the victim would have been diagnosed today. We do know the mode of death would have been obscured and accompanied by a list of phone numbers for counselling services.

A famous judge's final moments are described in the type of detail these days kept within the family: 'A few minutes before he died, the phlegm in his throat gradually accumulated, and his frame quivered'. An 'insanity expert' arrested after accepting payment from a rich Cuban widow for a favourable diagnosis of her son in his murder trial says: 'The mother is as crazy as the son.' It's not hard to imagine the excitement of the reporter who took down that quote.

The *Chronicle* is evidence that good, hard reporting can sit alongside shoddy work. It's also a reminder that journalists occasionally invent stories. Column inches need to be filled. Reporters are pushed into the sea of humanity and told not to return without a story. Sometimes they are given 'experiments' to conduct. In the late 1990s, a colleague of mine was sent onto the streets of Sydney with a handful of coins and a photographer. 'We just went to Martin Place and started dropping coins,' he recalls. 'I think the premise was how low would you go? Would you stoop for one dollar?'

One hundred years earlier the same dynamic played out in a New York City newsroom when a reporter was sent into the streets of Manhattan to survey hair colour. As can happen today, statistical rigour was sacrificed for narrative:

In the course of fifteen minutes' walk on Broadway he counted 200 women ... with hair ranging from medium brown ... to black. He passed only thirteen women of the pronounced blonde type. At the theatre the same evening he scrutinised fifty women within easy range and only six had light hair.

The thesis of the article was blondes were dying out. The reason for their imminent extinction was given by a Dr Beddoes of the Royal Infirmary in London, who 'arrived at the conclusion that in matrimony the brunette was preferred over the blonde in the ratio of three to two, and so gradually, but surely, through the selection of dark women for wives ... blondes become extinct'.

Hardly scientific, yet there is some strange power in this myth that has prompted journalists to retell it many times since. The debunking website snopes.com cites half a dozen examples foretelling the demise of blondes, the last of whom – according to one story – will die in 2202 in Finland. The meme exploded in 2007 thanks to the kerosene of Facebook. This time it was redheads, or gingers as they are known in some parts, whose death was greatly exaggerated. The story from Brisbane's *Courier-Mail*, 23 August 2007, was titled: 'Gingers extinct in 100 years, say scientists'. We picked it up on the Likeable Engine in early 2012 as a zombie story. As Dom explained earlier, a zombie is harvested from a news site's home page with pre-loaded shares. Mostly this happens when an old story is recirculated onto a home page through a 'most popular' module. Often the old story has been posted to a forum or message board and, because of its inbuilt shareability, is brought back from the dead.

Many stories about the demise of fair-headed people contain a modicum of scientific respectability and a dose of received wisdom. Redheads do make up a small percentage of global colouring, and the gene for fair hair is recessive so will generally lose out when brunettes and redheads mate. The propensity for fair-haired people – blondes or readheads – to suffer from skin cancer in an age of a depleted ozone layer, and the increasing ease of global intermingling are also cited as evidence for the blonde demise theory. Which is fine except that it is complete garbage. Geneticists do not say redheads or blondes will die out. Just because a gene is recessive does not mean it will disappear altogether.

Rethinking fakeability

The Share Wars team has never considered the veracity of shared stories. It was always the drivers within the narrative itself that interest us. But the explosion of fake news since 2013 has forced a bit of rethink. Take the redhead story, for example. The driver associated with sharing this story appears to be the Teaming instinct. Elements of the story appeal to our inherent tribalism and sense of identity, and also to our understanding of sex, life and death and our desire to leave a legacy. Each of us will die and most will be forgotten by the time our immediate descendants perish. The idea that our future world might not contain blondes and redheads prompts us to reflect on this legacy.

At Share Wars we also believe that sharing for the sake of humour is Teaming behaviour. Even though redheads have been portrayed in movies and TV as wild and alluring, poking fun at 'gingers' is sport for some. It is likely that a fair percentage of the sharing of the redhead story was driven by people who found it funny or used it to troll redheads in their networks.

The story itself is a bit of an albino, a Moby Dick. Since the advent of Facebook and the ability to accurately track

212

audience interaction with a product, marketers have constantly been trying to create campaigns that go viral. Success is elusive. Marketing messiahs such as Jonah Sachs and Seth Godin say brands need to be authentic to gain traction. But this particular fake story was based on information from the Oxford Hair Foundation, an organisation funded by Procter & Gamble, makers of hair dye among many other things. It seems the P&G marketers created a rare white whale and, as far as we know, no real harm was done apart from some hurt feelings.

Harmful or not, hoax news holds little appeal for journalist Erin Tennant, a truth seeker and a truth-teller. Mid-thirties, athletic and earnest, Tennant makes an even-tempered and determined reporter. He would have been a great detective. Expert at using Freedom of Information requests, Tennant is happy to play a long game if there is a story in it. He outwaits spin doctors and mandarins, studiously complying with demands for clarifying questions and then resubmitting information requests until he gets what he is looking for. As a journalist at ninemsn he always delivers an original story even if it does not always find an enthusiastic audience. Deterministic and irony-free, he is nicknamed the 'T-Bot', as in Tennant Robot.

On 3 May 2012, the T-Bot turned his curiosity to a story that seemed a little off-colour. It was a *Daily Mail* rewrite about a dentist removing all her ex-boyfriend's teeth in a fit of rage (yes, the same story Hal outlined in Chapter 4). It tweaked T-Bot's antennae. As he recounts, there was something weird about the quotes. They came off as frivolous given the horror of the act.

'The victim said, "Oh, yeah, when I got home I looked in the mirror, and I couldn't fucking believe it. The bitch had emptied my mouth." I thought that sounded like someone who is kind of annoyed about falling victim to a silly prank … he doesn't really comprehend what a grim situation he's in,' Tennant says.

The self-incrimination in the quotes by the dentist also struck Tennant as strange.

'She said, "I try to be professional and detach myself from my emotions, but when I saw him lying there, I just thought, what a bastard."

'You could only say those things if you had absolutely no regard for your professional reputation, let alone the risk of going to jail,' Tennant says.

That there were no photos accompanying the article and scant detail about any investigation of the incident also raised red flags. And once his suspicions were aroused, T-Bot swung into action.

His first call was to the *Daily Mail* journalist who had rewritten the story from the obscure *Austrian Times* via the mysterious Central European News Agency. Tennant asked the *Mail* for contact details for the sources or the Polish dental association. None were forthcoming.

Next Tennant used a Polish translator to compose an email to local police, who had no record of the incident. He then wrote to the Polish Chamber of Physicians and Dentists, which came back to him 'confirming it was bullshit'.

These were early days in the hoax news game, so Tennant's debunking story received worldwide coverage. Craig Silverman, resident hoax-slayer for journalism think-tank the Poynter Institute, wrote about Tennant's piece. Eventually most news sites removed their rewrites. But by then they had the page views in the bag. The damage was done.

The *Daily Mail* journalist responsible had to take his medicine in the form of a visit to the *Mail*'s ferocious editor-in-chief, Martin Clarke. But it was not the usual Clarke shellacking, according to a former colleague:

> Getting called into [Clarke's] office would give you shivers and trembles. But on this occasion, Martin apparently was calm, did not bollock the reporter, and just advised him softly not to share details outside the organisation. At times, such as this one, he could show his more human soft side, which does exist, despite reports to the contrary.
>
> And to be honest, not much wrong was done. The report came from a news agency, who you have to be able to trust. If they mess up too many times, then you learn not to trust them.

It is tempting for digital editors to look the other way – or not dig too deep – when this sort of material presents itself. Better to put it out there, harvest the page views and quietly remove the story afterwards if it turns out to be rubbish. Not a great way to treat your readers, but the data shows mass audiences do not care about hoaxes enough to shun an offending site. There appears to be no real penalty for publishing bullshit. Indeed, it is tempting to classify this as victimless crime.

Tennant does not think so. He spoke to the American Dental Association, which was concerned the story would deter people already scared of the dentist's drill from getting their teeth checked.

Just as the foundation of medical care is to 'do no harm', the primary role of journalists is to tell the truth. This includes doing the groundwork to separate fact from fiction, and not taking source material at face value. The first point of the Australian Journalists' Code of Ethics makes this explicit:

1. Report and interpret honestly, striving for accuracy, fairness and disclosure of all essential facts.

Laziness, a lack of time and a desire to increase page views are no excuses. 'Thou shall not lie' is an article of journalistic faith. To disregard it is to enter the realm of Hollywood, which plays by an entirely different set of rules. But there is no reward for checking a great story that happens to be bullshit.

Fake it up 2014

At the start of the Share Wars project in 2011, we predicted that the sharing of news through social media would change the industry for better. Our theory went that people would share valuable material because they wanted to present a better side of themselves on Facebook and Twitter. In simple terms, the audience is happy to click on the Kim Kardashian story but will not take the extra step of sharing.

Remember the unloved Lindsay Lohan car crash story? We are far more likely to share a story that has novelty, emotion or utility. As sharing drove an ever greater slice of audience, news organisations would divert resources away from Kim Kardashian to more important – more shareable – subjects. That was our simple and optimistic theory.

Something happened in 2014 to dent this optimism. An onslaught of fake news hit the internet, propagated through social media. In fact a whole industry had grown up around the creation of fake articles designed specifically to be shared on Facebook. Many of the offending mastheads are named to impart authority: *National Report*, *Civic Tribune* and *World News Daily Report*. Most have a professional look and feel. *National Report*'s article page resembles the *Huffington Post*. Its tagline 'America's No. 1 Independent News Source' is flanked by headshots of Republicans Ted Cruz and Sarah Palin. There are no obvious disclaimers. The headlines are believable and play to the biases of certain readerships. This sample from a single day in January 2015 is typical: 'Kids who know Santa is fake have higher IQs – study'; 'Obamacare pays for Octomom's new fertility treatments'; 'Joseph Kony gunned down by Seal Team 6, Obama takes credit'.

Somehow plausible, often amusing and always false, each headline comes with a targeted audience segment primed to approve – or disapprove – and share. Who among parents of Santa sceptics would not feel proud after reading the first headline? That pang is the instant of bias confirmation, the point at which scepticism dissipates. Clicking the Like button is a natural, almost frictionless, next step.

Once viral, these stories are commented on and shared mostly by people not in on the joke. *National Report*'s Kony story attracted 30,000-plus Facebook shares, which is more than most front-page stories from *The New York Times*. The monster sharers from *National Report* are in the millions. In late 2014, the site published a story about the Texas town of Purdon being quarantined after an Ebola outbreak. It was shared more than 1.5 million times, presumably by many people in a state of panic. This was sharing on a rare scale and Facebook was the accelerant. Bad news for our theory and no cause for optimism.

Breaking news versus faking news

While 2014 saw a tsunami of fake news engulf our Facebook news feeds, there were some in the media trying to plug their fingers and toes in the dyke. Various websites have been debunking rumours and urban myths since well before this phenomenon first emerged in a noticeable way in 2013. Snopes has been doing it since 1995. Reddit is another place where you can identify fake stories early in their life cycle. *The Washington Post*'s Caitlin Dewey has written that she spent 2014 debunking *National Report*'s fakes with 'exhausting frequency'. VICE News and The Verge has also published articles investigating the proliferation of fake news.

Sometimes *National Report* is portrayed as a fun-loving crew of japesters aiming barbs at Tea Party types, bigots and idiots. VICE has called it 'a darker, angrier version of *The Onion*': '*National Report* skewers mass media coverage of trending stories by dreaming up patently ridiculous news and passing it off as real. It pisses people off.'

One of the pissed off is Craig Silverman, the guy from the Poynter Institute who followed up Tennant's dentist story.

'There's absolutely no argument I can imagine that would suggest that there's some kind of social value in playing on people's fears and panic,' Silverman says. 'To take it to a level that ... becomes almost a public safety menace.'

The big question I had, as I started investigating the fake news phenomenon, was why. There is no obvious signpost to satire on *National Report*. It looks and quacks like a right-wing blog. So why was *National Report* churning out these widely shared fake articles but obscuring their satirical intent? I could understand trolls launching the occasional hoax but this was more systematic. Who was *National Report* sending up apart from the gullible? I was struggling to see a motivation behind this other than sport.

To answer *why*, I thought I needed to know *who*. Deciphering this was not straightforward. *National Report*'s bio page is littered with fake information. The Ebola story writer, Jane M. Agni, is also the author of a book titled *The States of Shame: Living as a Liberated Womyn in America*. The book does not exist. Agni's Facebook page is phantom. She writes for another spoof site called *Modern Woman Digest*, whose staff page also contains a list of obviously fake writers. Other *National Report* staffers include Barbara Bagwell, who won an award for 'Lady Journalism', and Cassidy Pen, a US Nicaragua veteran who documents 'the decay of Christian morals in his beloved America while sadly witnessing the rise of Satan's influence'. This would appear to be nonsense.

National Report's publisher is a digital cutout named Allen Montgomery, a man with no LinkedIn profile and a Facebook page that was started in January 2013. Only two images exist of Montgomery, a smug Ivy League type superimposed on different backgrounds – one a library and the other a glass-curtained, mid-rise building with an NR logo, presumably the *National Report* headquarters.

National Report came onto my radar when a story broke about the arrest of the UK's anonymous artist Banksy. This story's sharing triggers are straightforward: long-running mystery over identity of subversive artist is solved. Newsbreaking and Teaming are at work. One reason this type of story shares is because there is a certain amount of knowingness about Banksy. The graffiti artist's fans are a bit of a crew. I run a digital newsroom and this is just the type of story that fires up online journalists, people who love a meme and live on the social news site Reddit, the original source of so much viral news.

The story was written by Paul Horner, who used what may or may not be his real name and a headshot to provide an identity for the anonymous artist. You want to know how to spot a fake? One tactic is to look for the name Paul Horner in the story. Horner has quoted himself as a Facebook executive defending a Facebook subscription fee, as well as a 15-year-old arrested for calling a SWAT team on one of his video-game opponents (SWATing, as it is called). Both fake stories starring fake Paul Horners. *The Washington Post*'s Dewey says Horner sees his work as 'one part activism, one part fan fiction, and many parts subversive, absurdist comedy'.

In the *Post* article, Horner describes himself as a former cocaine-snorting, often-drunk mortgage salesman who quit his $20,000-a-month job for a stint as a search engine optimisation specialist in Hawaii before turning his hand to satire. His preferred targets are the religious/conservative right. Horner's proudest moment came when a story he wrote was cited as fact on FOXNews. The article was about how Barack Obama was using his personal wealth to fund a Muslim museum in Mississippi.

'Is *National Report* the fake news site, or FOXNews?' Horner asks in justifying his work. 'You decide.'

Attempting to verify Horner's biography as reported in *The Washington Post*, I searched 'Paul Horner Hawaii'. It turns out there *is* a Paul Horner in Hawaii but he is resort manager on Kauai. No mention of search-engine whispering skills. Page two of the search results yielded a story about a different Paul Horner who married his dog in San Francisco. This was more like our man. And there he was in one of his favourite zones, trolling the religious right and anti gay marriage lobby.

Horner's Facebook page is public and runs back to the late 2000s. It contains messages from schoolfriends in Minnesota. He has posted videos of stand-up comedy spots he did at a club called Copper Blues.

I searched for the club. It showed up on Google Street View as a two-storey 1990s glass and granite building in downtown Phoenix. I peered at the man in the videos, standing on a stage behind scores of illuminated beer taps. His face matched the hundreds of other Paul Horner pictures posted to Facebook, including the shot he used for the Banksy hoax. Check.

His routine contained jokes I saw him try out on Super Official News, his personal hoax sandbox site. Check.

The clincher came when I found a Facebook post showing a page from his middle-school yearbook. A young Horner appears in the centre of the page from Apple Valley Middle School's Year 8, 1993, Yearbook. On the same page is a child named Vinnie Kartheiser, the actor who played the villainous Pete Campbell in *Mad Men*. The Facebook commentary from Horner and his friends is just the type of conversation you'd expect from ex-schoolfriends of a famous person:

FRIEND: Wonder if he ever thinks of us …

HORNER: I was real good friends with Vinnie from 3rd grade up till 9th. When he got famous, I never heard from him again. I doubt he ever thinks of us or Apple Valley.

FRIEND: Money and fame can really change people. It seems as though it had the same effect on him. His parents really pushed him pretty hard at a young age for a career in entertainment and acting …

HORNER: Yeah, they pushed him real hard growing up. I remember we were going to do a talent show for school in 3rd or 4th grade. He wanted to be part of our 'air guitar' thing we were doing. He even practiced with us a bunch, but his parents wouldn't let him. He ended up doing a thing by himself singing in front of the school.

FRIEND: I feel bad that it affected your friendship so much. His parents were most likely driven by the money he would potentially bring in … He definitely had the charisma of a star even way back then.

HORNER: Vinnie's parents were already pretty well off. They pushed all of their kids hard. The parents were nice people, just wanted their kids to do well when it came to performing and acting.

The exchange convinced me Paul Horner was real. But I couldn't help thinking he was having a lend of his old school buddy. Horner's work reminded me of David Thorne, an early internet prankster who published the results of his trolling communications with neighbours and administrators. Thorne once famously tried to pay an overdue bill with a drawing of a seven-legged spider. The key to this pranking approach is the victim is unaware of the joke. A British satirist named William Donaldson did something similar in his 1980 book, *Henry Root Letters*, which writer Auberon Waugh rated as one of the great insights into British society at the time.

'The fake letters were sent to some of the most eminent people in the UK. Root … sometimes enclosing £1 or even £5 to ensure an answer, always in a friendly, enthusiastic manner, expounding his lunatic right-wing opinions and enlisting their support for various dubious proposals,' Waugh wrote.

Was there a William Donaldson behind this modern-day Henry Root? If Paul Horner was fake, this was a very thorough job. But these *National Report* guys are pretty good. In the only recorded interview I could find with Horner's boss, the very opaque Allen Montgomery described how the team set up a fake website and then generated social media buzz – presumably via fake accounts – from which to launch a hoax story about the use of food stamps to buy marijuana.

For a while I thought perhaps Horner and Montgomery were the same person. But there are subtle differences in the way they describe their work. Horner explains his philosophy of faking on one of his websites, Super Official News, in a section dedicated to tips for aspiring news satirists: 'Write your story about something positive or something you would like to see done, or making light of something you disagree with … Stories about celebrity deaths and evil stuff like that is just bad karma and it's not funny, unless it's about Justin Bieber.' (As a student of meme and sharing culture, Horner is, unsurprisingly, aware of the power of dead celebrity stories, whose sharing in our NIT model is driven by Newsbreaking > marking the moment.)

Horner is left-of-centre. His targets are mostly bigots. He counts his Bansky hoax as a tribute to the anonymous artist. Montgomery, however, sees everyone as fair game: 'There is no single political viewpoint motivating NR,' Montgomery has said. 'We are an equal-opportunity operation and everyone is a potential target.'

Both describe their output as satire. Horner views the content of his articles as the core statement; Montgomery describes *National Report*'s mission as far more over-arching: to help readers separate fact from fantasy by deliberately publishing misinformation. It is unlikely these details would diverge if they were the same person.

An interesting but disturbing theory began to emerge from the confusion I felt as I trawled the web for proof of the existence of these news hoaxers. If these fake stories – published by *National Report* and propagated on Facebook – were such enormous sharers, and the audience shares stories it values, did it follow that fake news was more valuable to this audience than real news? What if these stories did a better job in some ways than those from *The New York Times*? If quality is defined as 'fitness for purpose', were these stories of higher quality than those appearing in *The Guardian* and *The Washington Post*? What if the 'facts' part of news was actually far less important to readers than we in the media had always thought? Scary stuff indeed.

I was reminded of the time Hal and I were working on redesigning the Nine News website. We used elements of the Blue Ocean Strategy as a framework for our thinking. The Blue Ocean Strategy says businesses can create products that find entirely new markets by viewing their product feature set and the markets they are aimed at in radically different ways. By eliminating or reducing some features and improving or adding others, businesses can access a 'blue ocean' of opportunity, as opposed to the prevailing 'red ocean' full of incumbent 'sharks' thrashing over existing customers. Cirque du Soleil is a classic example. It eliminated animals and star performers from the traditional circus experience but added artistic music and dance presented within a unique circus-tent-like venue. For the first time, business people could take corporate clients to the circus. The Quebec-based troupe reinvented the circus in such a radical way that it could charge substantially more than other circuses.

Another case is the Australian brand Yellow Tail wines, which uncovered a latent market of US wine drinkers previously intimidated by features the wine industry had assumed were essential. Yellow Tail eliminated all the wine terminology around age, variety and provenance that other producers pasted on their labels as proof of quality. They offered sweeter, less complex wines in a bottle with a bright yellow kangaroo label. Suddenly American beer and spirits drinkers saw they had an alternative and Yellow Tail went on to become the highest-selling wine in the US.

When Hal and I sat down to reconsider the Nine News site, we assessed it against a number of features, including brand heritage, video storytelling and speed to publication. Not for a second did we consider 'truth' as a feature of news that could be improved on, reduced or eliminated. If news was defined as 'new information or a report about something that has happened recently' then truth was implicit. Others might look at that definition and decide it is not. There is also a pervasive belief that there is no such thing as truth, only different perspectives. But for now let us define truth as 'not bullshit'.

The overwhelming success of *National Report* and others suggests truth is not mandatory. Made-up news stories serve as a news analogue for part of the Facebook audience. People sharing fake stories are mostly Teaming and sometimes Newsbreaking, as was the case with the Ebola story. Because fake stories often have preposterous details buried in the final paragraphs, it is obvious many readers do not make it to the bottom before commenting and Liking. The purveyors of this content will tell you most people do not even read past the headline before sharing. They're merely reacting to the idea of the content because it pushes their buttons. Untrue news gives them an outlet. It is false but useful – unless of course your network is wise to the ruse, and then suddenly sharing it is a source of shame.

Meet a fake-maker

The man who calls himself Allen Montgomery says *National Report* is part of the solution. He sees himself in a public health role, inoculating users against future gullibility when they are called out by their networks for distributing fake news. The logic goes that a small dose of humiliation will create a better news consumer. (Tough break, Auntie Nora. Next time you'll think twice before clicking that Like button.)

I wanted to test this reasoning, and was intrigued by the digital cipher himself. To understand the fake news phenomenon I needed to talk directly to its master.

I call Montgomery just after Christmas 2014. We have agreed to a voice-only Skype call because he wants to maintain anonymity. I wait as the Skype avatar pulsates in the middle of the screen. I try to recall Paul Horner's drawl from a YouTube video at the Copper Blues club in case I can match it with the voice I'm about to hear. Unexpectedly someone materialises on screen. He has short, dark hair and wears a powder-blue polo shirt. He sits in a lounge room which I later find out is somewhere in southern California. A photograph of a sunrise is mounted on the wall behind him. This is Allen Montgomery. It is not Paul Horner.

'You are literally the first person that has seen my face as Allen Montgomery,' he says. 'I do my best to be very anonymous.'

Montgomery has reason to be cautious. He says he has received hundreds of death threats and that 'people try to find' him. Not long ago, someone did find him and published a picture of his house on Twitter. He was concerned for the safety of his wife and daughters.

Even the affable Canadian Silverman calls the *National Report* 'scumbags'. Passions run higher south of the border, particularly when you target those on the poles of heated issues. Fringe-dwellers are more likely to have guns. (I later mention my sighting of the scumbag-in-chief to Silverman. He immediately asks if I took a screen grab. I did not. 'He told me that we know someone in common,' says Silverman, who had spoken to Montgomery months earlier. 'I don't think there is any reason why he should be able to keep his real name out of it.')

I am interviewing Montgomery in the days following the *Charlie Hebdo* massacre in Paris. *Charlie Hebdo* and *National Report* do quite different things. One is a famous old left-wing satirical news magazine, the other is a hoax news site no one had heard of two years ago. However, it is a sobering time for anyone inflaming extremists through storytelling. Montgomery is most concerned about 'Joe Schmo militant guys', right-wing Timothy McVeigh types, not Islamic extremists.

'Once you get to the fringe, their beliefs are what they are. And if you insult them, it's cause for pain,' Montgomery says.

'I certainly would hate for something like that to happen over just screwing around online.'

But Montgomery is not just screwing around. Even though he still has a day job as a customer relationship management consultant to a magazine publisher, *National Report* is his passion after hours. It has grown into a substantial operation. His loose band of writers are comedians and satirists – not journalists – who pitch ideas and hone stories through group-sharing software. There are no editorial conference calls. The whole thing is done online so anonymity is protected. As Montgomery speaks about the site and its people, he sounds like any other digital media boss facing the usual personnel and product issues. Much of his time is spent recruiting: 'We're trying to increase the quality of our writing. We're not just trying to let anybody in that thinks they can tell a joke.'

New recruits cut their teeth at Montgomery's WIT (Wyoming Institute of Technology) site – a fake science–technology blog – before graduating to the big leagues of *National Report*.

I am surprised to hear Montgomery has just dealt with the departure of his superstar writer Paul Horner, whom he describes as 'your standard Hunter S. Thompson creative type … hard to figure out'.

'We had to let him go. He and I just had disagreements about some legal issues. There were plenty of other things that led up to it,' Montgomery says.

Horner has set up a new site called newsexaminer.net that mixes fake news with real news, a strategy Montgomery has been considering since it was suggested by his team. The idea is that the line between legitimate and phoney content is further blurred in the mind of the consumer. This move, however, would run counter to the concept of fake news as a public service, which Montgomery assures everyone is the key purpose of *National Report*.

'My site is a primer. We give you that first little taste of "Wow, I was just fooled by something that looked very legitimate. Maybe next time I should pay more attention to what I'm sharing and what I'm saying and what I'm believing",' Montgomery says.

Regardless of Montgomery's motives, his experience during the past two years has taught him much about virality. Even though he does not play by the most important rules of journalism, he has learned a lot of lessons in sharing. The first point he makes when I ask him for his secret sauce is that he and his colleagues have not 'worked out the formula' for sharing yet.

ALLEN MONTGOMERY'S TOP FIVE TIPS FOR MAKING A FAKE

1. Get the headline right

Montgomery says nailing the headline 'gets you most of the way there ... It has to grab your attention, obviously.'

2. Play to confirmation bias

National Report is expert in dishing out storylines people are keen to read because they are primed to believe them. Confirmation bias dictates that people favour information that reaffirms their beliefs. Montgomery describes the method as: 'We're going to tell you something we knew you wanted to hear already. Whether that comes from a place of your political ideology or your religious ideology or the kind of show you like to watch ... we want to confirm what you already had in mind.'

3. Business up front, party in the back

Following the playbook of *The Onion* – perhaps the most famous ongoing English-language satirical publication – Montgomery advises hoaxers to keep the first couple of paragraphs as plausible as possible. 'People generally quit reading at that point,' he says.

4. Target cult audiences

Look for pre-primed audiences aggregating around ideas they are passionate about. On a niche scale, *National Report* seems to dedicate disproportionate attention to Juggalos, the obsessive fans of the Insane Clown Posse hip-hop group, who only number in the 'tens of thousands' according to Wikipedia. At the other end of the scale, the site regularly 'gets the right wing all fired up' with anti-Obama stories.

5. Experiment

National Report publishes 'tons of things that don't go anywhere', Montgomery says. 'It's discouraging. You'll spend a lot of time on something that you think is just going to knock the socks off, and it falls on its face.' Montgomery says you have to dust yourself off and try something else.

I ask Montgomery why. Why does he work all day in a traditional media business as whoever he is and then suit up as Allen Montgomery at night? He says he's in it for his team, who are 'like a family'.

'The business model that I've created allows them to be extremely successful. Most people that are writers and creative types don't normally make a lot of money,' he says.

The business model is a straightforward advertising share: Montgomery keeps the revenue from the ads around the shell of the website and the writers collect revenue from the ads inside their article pages. At the height of the Banksy hoax, Horner claimed he was making $10,000 per day. At the average rate of $1 CPM (cost per 1000 ad impressions), and assuming there are four ads per article, he would have needed to attract 2.5 million page views per day. Montgomery confirms his writers can earn in this ballpark. He says that if they deliver five heavy hitters in a month they could bank up to $25,000. And the Banksy hoax was the heaviest of hitters. As for the boss, he pays himself a salary after deducting hosting, legal and image-rights fees.

'It's doing really well ... beyond my expectations,' he says. 'I'm certainly not rich. I live in southern California, so everything here is expensive.'

And in the other corner ...

Silverman lives at the opposite end of North America but, like Montgomery, has a job you could do from anywhere in the world. Journalist, author and entrepreneur, Silverman is a media man for the modern age, with clients in the US and

Europe, and an audience across the globe. He chooses to live in Montreal. ('I came here for journalism school and have been happy and lucky to stay.')

Silverman's house is a 10-minute walk from the warehouse office space he shares with designers, artists, editors and entrepreneurs in the Plateau district. There's a great soup and sandwich place, small design firms and a handful of start-ups. Google Street View shows a proliferation of bicycles, coffee bars and converted brick warehouses basking in the northern summer sun. But the real-time ambience as I speak to Silverman just two days into 2015 is decidedly grimmer. It is dangerously cold: minus 31°C with wind chill. There are no bicycles in the streets. People are ice-skating to their offices. Sometimes it gets so cold, Silverman says, your eyelashes freeze your eyes closed as you're walking to work.

Silverman has an eye for a good story – and a bad one, as it turns out. A decade ago, he started a blog called Regret the Error, which called out and corrected mistakes in journalism and was later acquired by the Poynter Institute. Since then, he has become an expert in journalism training and standards, working as a visiting professor at journalism schools across the US and Europe, writing a book also called *Regret the Error*, and producing policy and training modules for media organisations such as Al Jazeera. He has multiple income streams from his varied assignments but the major project is Emergent.com, his website that runs a constant tab on hoax stories and other contentious content published on the web and distributed mostly on Facebook.

The year 2015 is a growth year for fake news, and Emergent's stocks are rising with the tide. When a candidate story emerges above the noise of social media at the 10,000-share mark, Silverman lists it on Emergent with one of three tags: True, False or Unverified, along with a short description of the article's origin. Emergent is a close-to-real-time tool that alerts its readers early in the story cycle, sounding the alarm, Silverman says, 'when it's in that grey area … not just when you know it's not true'. There is value in this for journalists and media organisations, and Silverman is building a business around it. As a result, part of his time is spent sourcing seed funding to go along with the money he himself has invested.

Much of his time is spent at the coal face debunking hoax news. Every day Silverman makes his way up to the fourth floor, removes his cold-weather gear, sits at his desk overlooking another warehouse next door and starts wading into what he terms 'the mass of bullshit on the internet'. Silverman sifts this river of media sewage using a variety of feeds and dashboards, and posts anything suspicious that is gaining traction to Emergent.info. He then sets about verifying or debunking the report in what has become a never-ending game of digital whack-a-mole. The mole Silverman has been whacking as much as any other is *National Report*.

Montgomery, for his part, is a fan of Silverman's work but says he is fighting the wrong war. 'He can spend the rest of his life trying to shut down fake news sites, and they will just keep popping up,' Montgomery says.

I tell Silverman his nemesis sees them as working on the same problem – educating readers and journalists to be more discerning consumers of journalism – from different ends. It's an idea he rejects whole-heartedly.

'I actually think that he's probably smart in every area of his life except what he's doing here, where he's somehow convinced himself that this is okay,' Silverman says. 'I almost expected him to say … that in order for me to exist, he has to exist.'

Like Darth Vader and Luke Skywalker, I suggest.

'Yeah, it's like, "Oh, my God … Craig. I am your father." But honestly, I didn't know about this guy and his website six months ago.'

An interesting dynamic exists between these two hard-working young fathers living at opposite ends of North America. Neither operates as a traditional newsroom journalist but each is earning a living in the field of journalism – or in the case of Montgomery, a facsimile of journalism. Both are expert in virality and sharing. As with many media operations these days, their businesses rely on social media. Montgomery's primary audience is on Facebook and Silverman's is the media-savvy Twittersphere. (It's mainly hate mail on Twitter for Montgomery: 'Hey @TNROnline go fuck yourselves and your shitty unfunny website. You're literally damaging the country,' one critic tweeted.)

Silverman says he wants Facebook to turn off the traffic 'spigot' to *National Report*. This relatively simple move could kill off *National Report* and its ilk overnight. But that might not be the best thing for Emergent. Opposing Montgomery and his fake journalism has gained Silverman recent column inches in The Verge, VICE News and *The Atlantic*. *National*

Report provides much grist to the Emergent mill, and in nominating an enemy such as Montgomery, Silverman has found a demon to slay.

He is not mincing words, either. If *The Onion* is at the righteous end of the satire–hoax continuum, Silverman says *National Report* is at the scumbag end, playing to base cultural and racial stereotypes and fears. Silverman's stance against Montgomery and crew came about when American fear of Ebola was peaking and *National Report* ran the now infamous story of the quarantining of the town Purdon. Montgomery says the coverage, which included fake live updates and tweets from Purdon, was *National Report*'s *War of the Worlds* moment. Silverman says this was the point at which *National Report* stepped over the line and used its expertise in virality to create a public menace.

'They weren't commenting on the fact that the fear around Ebola was far greater than arguably it should be. What they were actually doing was stoking that fear. They knew by doing that, people would share these stories,' Silverman says.

'Because the human reaction – when there's uncertainty or a threatening situation – is to try to keep each other informed. When somebody who is already nervous about Ebola sees a story about a Texas town being quarantined, their first reaction is to get that out so other people understand this threat.' (Of course, in the NIT model this is classic Newsbreaking > Explaining behaviour.)

Silverman has no time for Montgomery's argument that his site is, as Montgomery puts it, a 'vaccine against disinformation'.

'He tries to say that he's exposing some of the right-wing biases ... out there, but he's not exposing anything because he doesn't admit what he's doing,' Silverman says.

'When people go to *National Report*, they think they're reading something real. There is absolutely nothing on the site to tell you that it's not real, so there's no point being made other than how much money he can make.'

CRAIG SILVERMAN'S TOP FIVE TIPS FOR SPOTTING A FAKE

1. Check the source
Follow the story to its point of origin. The source that is cited in the last article or tweet could be 10 degrees removed from the original. It usually only takes about five minutes of following links back to that point of origin. Once you're there, you can judge the quality of the actual source.

2. Look for exotic sources/language issues
Often when stories jump large geographic and language barriers, fake elements are inserted or misunderstandings occur.

3. Is it too good to be true?
If a narrative is too clean and smooth, there's a good chance reality has been warped.

4. Context can cause mistakes
True information can become false when it loses its correct context. A common example is mix-ups over war footage – when old footage is passed off as current or the wrong war zone is identified. 'When there was the conflict in Gaza last

year, there were plenty of videos and photos from Lebanon, from Syria, from Iraq, that people said were from the Gaza conflict,' Silverman says.

5. Do due diligence on websites

Start with the URL – is it a legitimate website? If the site is unfamiliar, read the About page. 'National Report's About page isn't too helpful. They disguise it pretty well. There are other sites of its ilk that will actually tell you that everything on the site is satire and it's not meant to be taken as real, so reading the About page on an unfamiliar source is important,' Silverman says.

These are the simple rules Silverman is teaching in newsrooms and classrooms across the US and Europe. Educating journalists in the identification of fake news is Silverman's main mission. After working with the Poynter Institute, his new sponsor is the Tow Center of Digital Journalism at Columbia University, which commissioned a paper from him that was published in February 2015 called 'Lies, damn lies and viral content – how news websites spread (and debunk) online rumours, unverified claims, and misinformation'. Silverman used his payment for the paper to fund the development of the software driving Emergent. It's a new twist on data journalism in which the journalist has access to their own unique data set.

'Data journalism, for a long time, has been about Access to Information requests, or it's been about getting governments and cities to put out open data,' Silverman says. 'We should also be building our own ways of gathering data that is proprietary and gives us insight that other people don't have. That's what I feel like Emergent has been doing for me. I see stuff other people don't. And you guys probably feel the same way.'

Home-brewed hoaxers

Just before Christmas 2014, two friends who do not know each other both told me about a fantastic stunt that took the craft beer industry down a peg or two. The brewers of Australia's most popular beer, Victoria Bitter, entered it into a craft beer competition re-badged as 'Vaucluse Bitter', and said it was created by two brothers from Byron Bay in subtropical northern New South Wales. Inexplicably, it won. The mainstream megabrewer had yanked the beards of the batch-beer posers. I think my two friends liked the fact the young inner-city trendies had been shown up as phoney. Neither really drinks craft beer but I cannot get enough of the stuff. It has been an education for me. Before craft beer, I did not understand how beer was made. I did not know what hops smelled like. These were dark times – the Dark Ages, except they knew all about hops in the Dark Ages. As much as my friends wanted the story to be true, I was dismayed by it.

Then something funny happened. My dismay pushed me to investigate the story. As I started my web search for Vaucluse Bitter, I somehow hoped to prove the story was fake: confirmation bias at work. The first result was from the *Betoota Advocate* – a bloggy news site – headlined 'VB goes undercover to win Surry Hills craft beer festival'. I started reading.

ALL YOUR FRIENDS LIKE THIS

> Carlton & United Breweries, a subsidiary of Foster's Group in Melbourne, have today confirmed that the winner of last month's Sydney Craft Beer Festival was in fact one of Australia's oldest and highest-selling beers – Victoria Bitter.
>
> The undercover infiltration of the October 24th festival took out number one place by an undeniable margin, which in turn embarrassed the entire craft beer community of Australia.

I thought it read more like a press release than a conventional news story. It needed a punchier lead. I kept reading until I hit the quotes from one of the craft beer judges, Banjo Clementé. The name seemed too hip to be true.

'It is just so typical of these big corporations. They couldn't cop the idea that our microbreweries might begin to compete with them,' Clementé said. 'They even grew their beards out, they looked the part. It's disgusting to see the lengths these corporate pigs go to to keep us down.'

Strong words from the sulking and embarrassed judge. The quotes from VB proprietor SABMiller's spokesman were even better:

'It just goes to show how much of a joke this microbrewery "culture" is … We won this round, and we will win again. This craft beer bullshit is just a phase.'

As the T-bot observed, one key to unlocking a fake story is the quotes. While you could imagine an apparent media novice such as Clementé shooting his mouth off, a big-liquor PR person was unlikely to be so injudicious. In reality, the spokesman's tone would have been far more conciliatory.

Why stick the boot in when the hipsters had already done it themselves?

Unlike Montgomery's gang of 'media misfits', the two men behind the *Betoota Advocate*, which is named after a western Queensland ghost town, are journalists. Or ex-journalists, as they believe. Until now they have stayed behind their pen names, Clancy Overell and Errol Parker. But the *Betoota Advocate* is taking off and it looks like there's a future in it. Overell and Parker reveal themselves as Archie Hamilton and Charlie Single, two graduates of my alma mater, Charles Sturt University, Bathurst, New South Wales.

We meet in a pub in Alexandria in Sydney's inner south, just the type of place that would have served Vaucluse Bitter. Hamilton is a big fellow with a big beard, 1940s-style short-back-and-sides and a booming FM radio news voice. Single is slighter, more quietly spoken, with long blond hair and an acerbic edge. Both have emerged disillusioned from their first stints in journalism. Hamilton grew tired of the FM radio news production line. Single lost his job at the *The Canberra Times* in a wave of redundancies and it hit him quite hard.

In something of a surprise, they have suddenly found themselves making a decent living by writing fake news. Facebook is driving most of the audience but 15 to 20 per cent of people are coming directly to their home page: a statistic that has Hamilton and Single scratching their heads.

'I don't know why, but people in my folks' generation will log on to news services each morning,' Hamilton says.

'If they want to know what's happening in the news, they'll go in via the tablet or the computer and look it up. There's no need for Facebook.'

They are seriously perplexed. Perhaps they need to hire an ethnographer to follow baby boomers as they make their digital way through their days.

On Silverman's satire-to-fake-news continuum, the *Betoota Advocate* is in *The Onion*'s territory. Unlike Montgomery, they are not concealing their identities for safety reasons but because they think they might hurt their chances in conventional journalism in the future. The closest thing to hate mail they receive, Hamilton says, is the odd 'sternly worded email'.

'It's Australia,' says Single. 'We're not going to be dragged out of our office and murdered in the street.'

Team *Betoota* has already enjoyed major success. In addition to the Vaucluse Bitter hoax, their biggest hitters have been an article about US playboy Dan Bilzerian being denied an Australian visa, a story about the TV brothers Karl and Peter Stefanovic drinking too much at their family Christmas get-together, and an item about a parking cop that earned them a spot on ABC TV's *Media Watch* after Channel Nine followed it up. They already have a good track record in creating shareable content and a few theories about what makes a story share.

Just as *National Report* and BuzzFeed have figured out, they say the most important component is the headline. Sounding just like an old-school subeditor, Single says you need to convey the essence of the story in seven to nine words.

One of their most shared stories exceeded that word count but worked just the same: 'A mature-aged student has gone an entire lecture without asking a question.' Anyone who has been to university knows what that means. No need to read further.

While that headline is obviously satirical, Hamilton says the best have an air of plausibility. The drunk Stefanovics story was assembled around pictures from the brothers' Instagram channels. Karl Stefanovic comes across as a party guy, so a story about his riotous drinking games at Christmas was not much of a stretch.

Single and Hamilton also use confirmation bias in their satire. Single calls it 'a gift to the state of mind' of the audience, an offering many find difficult to refuse.

The story about Dan Bilzerian is a case in point. Bilzerian is a very rich ex-navy, trust-funded playboy known as the 'King of Instagram' for publishing pictures showcasing his outrageous lifestyle in the Hollywood Hills. A quick scan of his account reveals countless images of women in lingerie, some holding guns and others with messages such as 'Property of DB' written across their backsides. Bilzerian is a 'hot button' who fires people up, says Hamilton. Loved by some, hated by many and leaving few indifferent, Bilzerian is perfect sharing fodder. Most who commented on Hamilton's article were not in on the joke, despite obviously made-up quotes from Bilzerian such as: 'I don't give a fuck – Australia looks like shit anyway. I'd prefer to stay at home with my cat and sleep with women that I hate.' The first comment on the article is typical: 'No loss ... this man is a pig.'

Hamilton and Single know they need to keep on their toes. Today's hot button is tomorrow's cold drink of water. They are constantly scanning the major news sites for trending subjects and celebrities. They know that the editors of these websites are themselves using telemetry to gauge audience interest in real time. Then they put their spin on the topic of the moment and send it out to Facebook, by far their biggest distribution channel.

As I speak to Single and Hamilton, the *Betoota Advocate* is already supporting them financially after only 100 days in existence. They joke they'll move into hospitality or construction if Facebook turns off the tap. To that extent, they find themselves in the same predicament as *National Report*. As we wind up our conversation I ask Single about the mission of the *Betoota Advocate*. He says something that could have come from the mouth of Montgomery.

'The purpose is to pretty much make the line between what's real and what's not even blurrier,' Single says. 'It's almost, in a way, trying to make sure all the bigger [media] players in the world … constantly ask themselves are they heading down our path?'

It is an absurdist's explanation for his reason for being. I think the lesson for mainstream media – and marketers – is different. What we observe in the *Betoota Advocate* is two young journalists entirely dedicated to creating shareable content and experimenting every day with stories that must flourish in the Facebook news feed if they are to pay their way. It has forced Single and Hamilton to focus sharply on the topics that matter to people.

Occasionally they do not realise their own strength. In late December 2014, the *Betoota Advocate* apologised for a story about how animal welfare group the RSPCA had sanctioned dog fights in Queensland.

'We were making a comment about how Queensland is still the cowboy state and how there were still dogfights in Queensland, which there are,' says Hamilton, a Queenslander.

'And we wrote a story about how the RSPCA was ... going down a new path by providing vets at dog fights to minimise risk.

'They were upset with us, understandably. We didn't realise that a story that far-fetched would be believed.'

Single says a Queensland politician described them as old burnt-out journalists. 'And we thought, "Yep, we're burnt-out journalists at 24."'

They later changed the story to say that the vets were part of a government scheme and issued an apology with a link to the RSPCA's fundraising site.

Of course, they can ignore many of the other conventions of journalism, but Single and Hamilton do not see themselves as journalists any more. By revealing their identities, they reckon they have burned their boats. I'm not so sure. I think both could return to mainstream journalism with valuable insights from the Facebook frontier. It is not that long since Single arrived at his desk at *The Canberra Times* to find an orange envelope containing the details of his redundancy. Now he is a half-owner and editor of a publishing business that has about twice the reach of the capital's newspaper.

'There are millions of people every week who are reading our stories,' says Single, sounding as if he scarcely believes it himself.

And that's the power of the Facebook news feed for those who understand the drivers of stories that flourish there. It is not as easy to do this with real content, and the conventions – in particular, headline styles – are constantly evolving. The moral of this story is not that journalists or marketers should make stuff up. But in being aware of hot topics, in understanding how the audience is primed, in mining knowledge gaps and stitching them into pithy headlines, and in identifying and emphasising the narrative elements that drive Newsbreaking, Inspiring and Teaming, journalists can boost their chances of reaching those millions.

These are the lessons people like Montgomery, Silverman, Single and Hamilton bring back from the sharing frontier.

Chapter 9

Arminland

By Hal Crawford

There's a line in Joseph Conrad's novel *Heart of Darkness*, near the beginning, about how all the world's oceans are connected in one big waterway. We have named parts of the waterway, imposed a series of artificial divisions on it, but actually it is unbroken. I feel that way about the stories told by news organisations. Every story is connected to every other story, and it's only our need to understand by clumping events into pieces that requires us to stop writing and wrap things up. This makes every ending more or less unnatural: something cadet journalists feel painfully as they try to end their articles. Older practitioners know better than to fuss with a final paragraph: a good story can be cut from the bottom, and where you end is arbitrary.

Tapping into the unending flow of stories is how newspapers and TV bulletins get filled up. To children it can seem miraculous that every day brings precisely 30 minutes of TV news. They assume that the bulletin or newspaper is a reflection of the world – 'All the news that's fit to print', to quote *The New York Times* – and are amazed that what happens in the world is always so conveniently sized. Of course they have it the wrong way around. It is the world as depicted in the news that is reverse-engineered to fit its container. Old media editors start with a number of minutes or pages, usually determined by the needs of advertisers, and then dip into the unending ocean to fill their vessels.

This is forgotten in any number of investigations into the future of journalism in a digital world. A common question at panels and conferences is: 'How will quality journalism be funded?' Seen through the lens of shrinking newspaper revenue, the view of the world implicit in this question – that there is insufficient money for proper reporting – seems to make sense. The earning density of display advertising online is less than that of printed ads. The sum of revenue from all the display ads in *The Sydney Morning Herald* on one random Friday in 2014 came to $660,000, based on the paper's standard rate card. With average circulation of 122,000 copies and readership of 534,000 (June 2014, Roy Morgan), at standard rates the newspaper was pulling in more than a dollar a reader. A digital news portal serving more than five times as many readers brings in half that on its display ads – just over 10 cents a reader – an order of magnitude less.

No amount of optimism can change the reality that profitable digital newsrooms are smaller than their old media counterparts. The depressing conclusion is that democracy will crumble, wrongdoers go unpunished and the ignorance of the masses pass for wisdom.

If plump newspapers and 30-minute TV news bulletins were the only vehicles of truth there might be something in this. But they are not. Like the kid and the TV, we have become so used to the familiar formats of news that we think there is something God-given in their forms, something that actually represents the entire world. If we can't fund them, we won't be able to cover everything. Terrible things will happen.

At the bottom of this gloomy view is the assumption that in the past all the important stories were covered.

That's not right. It's a straight-up case of survivor bias, our tendency to see only what is, forgetting about all that there could be. We know about Watergate and Abu Ghraib and we thank God we have nailed the bad guys. We picture the 'miracle on the Hudson' and are inspired by the skill of pilot Chesley Sullenberger. Yet countless untold stories – the hidden abuses and the unknown heroes are never entered in our mental ledgers.

It's clear that there are many more stories in the world than we have the opportunity to tell, and some of the unspoken ones are as important and interesting as anything that sees the light of day.

The lion and the lamb.jpg

On 11 January 2011 a remarkable photo was submitted to ninemsn news. The photo shows a green frog sitting on the back of a swimming snake. The snake is floating just in front of a submerged fence with its head rearing out of the water and its long body curved in serpentine motion. The frog is perched a few feet back from the head. It is an image from the great floods that hit Queensland at that time.

The story, which really goes no further than the simple observation of prey hitching a ride on predator, has many of the features of shareability as laid out in SENT. It's simple and concrete, surprising – a perfect reverse – and something about it is hopeful. It sits firmly in the Inspiring box of NIT, and for extra power, its actors are animals. The 'frog on the snake' could have been a freeze-frame from one of Aesop's fables, and it was bound for success.

The sender was 'Armin Gerlach' from Queensland. A cadet journalist, Anne Lin, interviewed Armin by telephone and wrote up the story. Later that day I called Armin too, because I thought the story would become big and I wanted to make contact and hear his voice.

Armin was pleasant and reasonable, but not overly talkative. He had written his occupation as 'computer technician'. He didn't try to shake me down for money or become evasive. He said he had heard of things like this before, where animals banded together in a flood, even natural enemies like foxes and rabbits. I didn't ask him why he had sent the picture in. It seemed obvious: he had witnessed something amazing and wanted to share it. He had named the image file 'the lion and the lamb.jpg'.

The next day, after the article had been viewed several hundred thousand times, we were called by international newspapers and picture agencies wanting to know how they could contact Armin so they could get the rights to the picture.

By the terms of the ninemsn submission process, copyright of a submitted picture belongs to ninemsn, but it seemed to me that this provision was to cover use by ninemsn and here was a possibility for Armin to benefit from his generosity to us. He had witnessed a small but extraordinary event – a good old-fashioned portent.

We contacted him again and he gave us permission to give out his contact details to the picture agencies. The story and photo appeared in several British newspapers; I have no idea how much money Armin received for the rights but I don't think it would have been a huge amount.

That would have been it but for the sharing: within 24 hours the frog-snake became the most shared piece of content on ninemsn up to that time. More than 54,000 people Liked, commented or shared it on Facebook. It's impossible to tell how many emailed it, but people arriving directly at the page (and not from the ninemsn home page, the usual traffic driver) accounted for 278,000 of its total of 619,000 page views.

It stood clear out of the crowd – the next most shared story up to then, David Thorne's attempt to pay a bill with a drawing of a spider, had had a share count of 23,000. Even within the flood stories, we had a similarly good story that failed to reach the same heights: a woman who returned home after the waters had receded and found a cow on her roof. She had sent us the surreal image of the marooned beast calmly looking down at the camera. That article stood at 7500. As another point of context, our article about Osama Bin Laden's death in 2011 had a share count of 6000. The frog-snake was something extraordinary. It was something that people really wanted to share. I felt compelled to investigate.

The plot thickens

The digitisation of the world is not so advanced that many individuals have left a particularly long or interesting digital trace online. So it was without a whole lot of hope that I plugged 'Armin Gerlach' into a search engine.

Immediately I hit a snag. I'd overlooked the reason I was looking up Armin in the first place. Armin was now known to the world as the witness of the frog on the snake – the signal was blown out. This 'Armin Gerlach' dominates pages and pages of search results. All that aggregation, all that paraphrasing of a few sparse facts on the barest frame of a story, and all because of that picture. I clicked through page after page until, about to abandon the search, something interesting showed up.

It was a PDF of a legal essay about the use of juries in Australian courts. I downloaded the document and found a reference to the case *Gerlach v Clifton Bricks Pty Ltd*, which had gone to the High Court. The essay summarised the issues: the case had originally been about compensation for a back injury at work, and the plaintiff Gerlach had at the last minute objected to its being heard before a jury. One of his grounds for objection was that the jury would be prejudiced against him because he had a criminal record.

At that moment my perception of both the frog-snake and Armin shifted. The rotund, benign computer technician in my head took on a different shape. I did some more searching, found the High Court transcript and judgements. Full name of plaintiff: 'Armin Herbert Gerlach'. Eminent High Court judges talking about the district court judge who agreed with Armin that a jury wasn't a good idea. Some of them were down on this judge. It wasn't the only time Justice Christie would get an official ticking off. He suffered from being a straight talker. For example, he once told some dodgy nightclub bouncers who had appeared before him they needn't bother applying for bail, as he wasn't going to grant it. You can't do that if you're a judge. You have to listen to the evidence, then apply the law. You can't pre-judge people just because they behave like idiots in the dock. You listen first, then you deny bail.

Armin versus the brick company wasn't that kind of issue. This was a civil case: a man with a bad back who'd been waiting nine years for his case to come to court. Nine years. On the final Friday before the week he was scheduled to appear he filed a petition to have the jury dismissed. He couldn't afford the motels for the witnesses. He had a criminal record.

So Judge Christie agreed with him, just – he described it as 'line-ball' – and the case was heard before a different judge without a jury. That judge awarded Armin $390,000 for the back pain, because the brick company had made him drive a forklift with solid tyres. The judge found evidence that Armin had already had the back problem before the solid-tyred forklift, nevertheless he gave him the money. Clifton Bricks decided that wasn't fair and appealed the matter and eventually it wound up in the High Court, where the five sitting judges decided 3–2 that even if dispensing with the jury was wrong, that was not enough to order a retrial and do the whole thing over again. Armin would keep the money. High Court judge Michael Kirby was in the minority; he thought juries were very important and that there were grounds for a retrial. He suggested Christie's discretion was skewed by his strong personal views that civil cases should no longer be heard before juries, given their substantial cost and length.

Here, just for a moment, the picture of the frog riding on a snake intersects with the legal history of Australia. Kirby retired in 2009. He is an inspirational figure if you happen to hear him speak. He tended to disagree with his colleagues on the bench. According to legal commentators, in fact, he disagreed more than any other High Court judge before or since. Why did he think juries were important? Because that's the way the Australian legal system is built: if you are trying to decide a question of fact, they are the default position. It's not up to the trial judge to throw out this ground wire back to the public just because he doesn't like dealing with people who know nothing about the law. As Kirby said: 'Absolute discretions are a form of tyranny.' He also pointed out that it was widely held that juries are hostile to work-related injury claims. A jury might have taken a dim view of Armin and his back pain. Armin certainly thought so.

But Kirby did not carry the day. There had been no jury, that was fine, and Armin got to keep his money. The High Court judgement was handed down about two decades after he had been driving that blessed forklift. Other details emerge from the case. Armin had got into the booze and drugs after his back went on him, and he spent 1993, 1994 and 1995 in jail. That's a long time. That's a bachelor degree in jail. I wanted to know what he had done, exactly.

Investigating Armin

You can't just look up someone's criminal record in Australia – you have to be a relevant organisation or the actual individual. In the US, no problem – it's like checking a library catalogue. In Australia it's deemed a good idea to prevent previous crimes from ruining the lives of criminals by not allowing any old member of the public to find out about them. The same logic could be applied to court cases, particularly before a verdict is delivered. I don't buy it, because there is provision for convictions to become 'spent' and therefore erased from the catalogue. What you have is a situation where notorious crimes and criminals are remembered, through the media, but perhaps equally heinous acts go invisible because the junior court reporter decided to attend Courtroom 1 instead of Courtroom 2.

My thinking on Armin at this point was that he had had a rough patch – 'a somewhat wild life', as he stated on his neglected Bebo social networking page – but did that have to define his whole life? I hoped not. One of the central ideas of Share Wars is that what people aspire to is incredibly important. Public truth is as worthy as private truth. Aspiration is big and beneficial and helps form societies that are worth being part of. What people admire has a massive effect on what comes to be, even if they are not privately faithful to their ideals. Armin's life might have something in it that showed the importance of public aspiration over private impulse.

So I found Facebook Armin, and Bebo Armin and then all the appearances he makes in the specialist legal databases. Facebook Armin matches up with all the other Armins – his daughter's name was part of his Hotmail address and she is one of his Facebook friends. He has sons as well, and they are Facebook friends also. He is friends with a German guy called Bernd Schmidtke and they converse in German. I suppose Armin may have been born there. There is also a verification that Armin left school in South Australia in 1972, which I think ties it all together. That makes Armin 58 or 59 years old, which puts him in the right zone to be the Armin Herbert Gerlach of the High Court case. He would have been about 29 when he was driving the forklift; enough time, if he'd been labouring since he left school, to have developed a bad back.

The unfortunate thing about Bernd Schmidtke is that, unlike Armin's, his name is common. Bernd, a form of Bernhardt, was one of the top 55 boys' names in Germany in the second half of the 20th century, and Schmidtke is a German form of 'Smith'. A German telephone directory lists 28 Bernd Schmidtkes.

One of these Bernd Schmidtkes was kidnapped by Soviet agents at a Berlin subway station in 1955. That boy was nine years old and fell victim to a cruel trick. The story is that Bernd's family had escaped from the East before the wall went up, and the Communists wanted them back. One day East German relatives sent the Schmidtke children a message to come and collect their Christmas presents. Berlin at that time was a tense, divided city that the Allied forces had carved up into zones. If you stepped into the wrong zone, you were subject to whoever owned that area. As soon as Bernd and his sisters walked onto the platform, which was technically part of the Soviet zone, a burly woman in a coat grabbed him and spirited him off. The sisters got away, back to the safety of the footpath, but little Bernd was gone. The Soviets had reclaimed one of their own.

Armin's friend graduated from high school in 1967, which makes him almost but not quite the same age as the kidnapped Bernd. Back then many German high schools hung on to their students until they were 19, so in the best-case scenario Armin's Bernd was born in 1948. Kidnapped Bernd was born in 1946. Two years might as well be a century. Not the same person. Just another one of the meandering brooks the frog-snake took me down. Nevertheless, the picture of Bernd crying in his cap and suit on the Berlin station platform is something I haven't forgotten.

So I knew from Facebook that Armin wears blue singlets, and has faded tattoos, close-cropped hair and a beard. He lives in a small town in northern Queensland and he repairs computers. I thought he probably bought the house with the money from the brick saga. But it isn't the only time he is mentioned in the legal record. Here's a summary of Armin's history as recorded in disparate state and federal databases:

ALL YOUR FRIENDS LIKE THIS

- The crime that landed him in jail: committed some time after 1985 and before 1992, involving drugs. Probably drug dealing.
- The Clifton Bricks case as mentioned. Armin sued for workers' compensation and his lawyers pulled a legal swifty on the opposition by asking for no jury a day before the trial was to start. Judges noted inconsistencies in his evidence but gave him the money.
- A work tribunal case regarding a man (A. Gerlach) who dishonestly tried to get a redundancy payment out of a company, and failed.
- A Centrelink case where the dole was stopped to Armin because he moved from Canberra to another area (the Queensland town). He successfully pressed for the payments to be made in arrears.

There is one more case in the record. It deserves special mention.

Early on the morning of 17 August 2000, two police officers responded to an emergency 000 call about a house fire in the Canberra satellite town of Queanbeyan. When they arrived at the house it was well alight. The officers were brave: they didn't wait for the firefighters, but went in and found two boys trapped by the flames in the hallway. One of the boys had a bleeding head. They carried both boys outside. Looking for a garden hose, one of the cops saw a 5-litre petrol can on top of a car in the garage. It was lying on its side and had a burning cloth wick stuffed into it. The other cop got a

258

garden hose and squirted the can down the driveway away from the house. Then the fire crew arrived and started hosing everything down.

One can imagine the mayhem and panic at such a scene. Modern houses burn quickly, because of the plastics inside. They also stink for the same reason; the smoke is toxic and hard to get out of your nostrils. It was still dark. The boys were yet to be treated and there was also a stricken eight-year-old girl outside, the boys' sister. It was she who had called in the fire.

The officers knew this was a crime scene already, because of the petrol can, and then the girl said: 'I saw my father light a car in the garage and then light the house and I saw him run away.'

The boy with the bleeding head said: 'My dad shot me in the head two times ... with a big shotgun ... My mum is dead ... I saw my dad slash her up.'

The boy was correct: he had been shot in the head. When they got him to the hospital, they found two .22 bullets that had not penetrated his skull. What was apparent to the police was that this was a classic domestic tragedy: a murder–suicide involving an unsuccessful attempt to kill the children and burn the house down. Going on what the children said at the scene and at the hospital a short while later, it was a reasonable assumption that the father had done it. 'Daddy lit the fire and I hate him,' said the little girl. She also mentioned that a man called 'Tim' had been at the house the previous evening. Tim had 'settled everything down'.

At the burning house there was nothing to be done except wait for the firemen to put out the flames, and when they had finished, the place was a sopping black mess. They found two bodies under the collapsed roof. They were Joseph McNally and Adelia Williams, the children's parents. The corpses were burnt, but it wasn't the fire that had killed them. Joseph had been shot in the head several times with a .22, through a cushion. Adelia had been shot in the head, stabbed, and strangled with a pair of socks tied around her neck. Both had their hands and feet tied, their hands behind their backs. So not suicide. And not domestic.

Forensically, the scene was a washout because of the smoke and the water. In the whole place they found just a single fingerprint – on the petrol can. As details came out over the next few days, particularly about the tied hands and feet, suspicion fell on 'Tim'. This man, Timothy Paul Villa, was a drug supplier to the dead parents. They owed him money, and according to one of his associates, he had fired a shotgun at their house in a drive-by 'reminder' a few weeks earlier.

One of the things that convicted Villa and put him away for life was the evidence of Armin Herbert Gerlach. Villa had tried to sell Armin a sawn-off gun and amphetamines, and while doing this, he had said of that August evening and the house on Barracks Flat Drive: 'It all went wrong, it wasn't meant to happen that way.'

Armin also stated in evidence that he was interested in neither the drugs nor the weapon.

So Tim Villa went to trial and told a story about a Maori man who had been at the Barracks Flat Drive house, and no one believed him. He knew too much about the crime, and he talked. He talked to Armin, he talked to other people. Once, on a bugged phone call to a mate, he referred to Adelia's hands having been tied up with telephone wire. His mate picked up on it immediately, and asked him how he knew. He replied that the police had told him. But the police hadn't told him – they didn't know. At that point they had assumed Adelia's hands had been tied up with cord cut from a Sega game controller, the same way her feet had been tied up. After listening to the phone call, they tested the cord on her hands and found it to be telephone wire.

Now Tim Villa is under special protection in prison. He had been getting bashed as a member of the general prison population – maybe because of what he did to the kids. He lost the appeal against his conviction and life sentence in 2005. Interestingly, the fingerprint on the can was never identified – it didn't belong to Villa. I don't want to imply he is innocent; there is an overwhelming case that Villa committed the crime. But it's weird what the kids said. I guess that eight-year-old really did hate her father.

Armin revealed

Armin's house is ramshackle. He tells me on the phone I don't need to know the street address – he's right. You drive a few hours north of Brisbane, you cross the railway tracks in this little town, and you see the 'Computer Shop' sign. That's his place. The 'Parking Area' sign points to an expanse of dirt.

When I walk in through the open gate, a middle-aged man with short grey hair and a fair-sized stomach is bent over something behind a patio bar. He straightens up.

In person, Armin is a lot like his digital trace. There's plenty there, but it's inscrutable. He has 'old bikie' written all over him: a trimmed goatee and a guarded air that feels like it could blossom into outright defiance at any moment. It doesn't. He's just a guy mending computers in an out-of-the-way Queensland town.

'Need to keep the flyscreens shut, up here,' he says as he leads me into his office. I close the screen door behind me. Every surface in the office is covered with computer parts: chips on green circuit board, eviscerated hard drives, connected and unconnected boxes and monitors. The profusion is the perfect cover for surveillance equipment; I wonder if he is recording us.

Armin was born in 1955 in Wixhausen, Germany, and came to Australia with his mother and brother when he was nine. He didn't speak a word of English.

'As a kid I was always done out as the Nazi,' he says. 'But the Australians, they didn't know what freedom was. They were always kowtowing to authority.'

Not Armin. As we talk it becomes clear that resisting authority has been one of the main activities of his life. Later on, after he's warmed up, he tells me the story of a small legal victory that I've thought about since. Its pointlessness strikes me as significant.

I was driving my wife's car and I was stopped by the police.

It's a Mercedes, they probably thought I was a drug dealer.

They stopped me and the policewoman asked:

'Is this your car?'

'No.'

'Who does this car belong to?'

'A woman in Canberra.'

'Does she know you have it?'

'Probably not.'

'Please step out of the car, sir, we are going to search it.'

So the police find this ornamental Chinese knife, about this long, in the dash that someone gave me. And then they find out that the car belongs to Marie Gerlach.

'Who's Marie Gerlach?'

'My wife.'

'Why didn't you say?'

'You didn't ask.'

So they charged me with possessing an offensive weapon.

We go down to the station and I am arguing with the duty officer, and he gets so sick of the whole thing. He picks up the knife by the handle and he holds it over the bin:

'I am going to drop this knife into this bin and we are going to forget all about this,' he says.

And I say: 'If you drop that knife I am going straight to the ombudsman and I am going to lodge a complaint.'

So they had to charge me. [On the day of the trial] I wrapped up a whole lot of kitchen knives in a towel and I took them to the courthouse. I produced them in evidence. 'Are they offensive weapons too?'

The judge agreed with me. The police said I could pick up the knife from the station. I said, 'Why can't I have it right now?'

The judge looks at me, and then he says:

'Just give him his knife.'

Armin's contradiction is that he loves rules – he would go to court over and over for rules – but he won't condemn his own past. In a life where so many things went wrong, he loves things to be right.

Everything that Armin tells me leads not to an ending but to another story that should be investigated. His grandfather Herbert was in the Luftwaffe and was killed by a bomb in Eastern Europe. His father, another Herbert, joined the Hitler Youth and was caught by the Russians at the end of the war. As a 14-year-old, Armin's father was sent east as a prisoner of war, and came back four years later an alcoholic and a wild man. Uncle Ziggy worked for Colonel Gaddafi, protecting the oil lines. His grandmother once ate human flesh.

Bernd Schmidtke? No, Uncle Bernd is quiet and straight. He was never kidnapped by the East Germans.

Armin has an ordered mind. He doesn't leap to unsupported conclusions. He doesn't call me 'mate', and his stories don't ring false. He doesn't mind being asked about anything – his crime was selling amphetamines, he went to Goulburn jail – but he won't tell me the name of his old bikie club.

The image of the burned house in Queanbeyan occurs to me. I ask Armin how he met Tim Villa, looking at his face to see if the name makes an impact. Nothing.

'He called me out of the blue and tried to sell me drugs and things,' he says.

I ask him about that morning, when the kids were found and the house was on fire. Did he see it?

'This is Queanbeyan – I think everyone went and had a look,' he says.

Why did the children try to blame their father for a crime committed by another man?

He doesn't know.

We talk about jail, we talk about the police, his children, his failed marriage, Clifton Bricks – 'they were like my family' – about the courts, never pleading guilty, never giving in, about going to the High Court, about drugs, about the shop he had, the boarding house, non-smoking laws, leaving Canberra under threat of death, ocean liners, Adelaide and his own natural ability.

At the end of the conversation, I ask him about the picture of the frog on the snake.

'I just want to know: why did you call it "the lion and the lamb"?'

For a moment it's clear Armin doesn't know what I am talking about.

'Is that what it's called?' He smiles. 'That's the thing about that photo,' he says. 'I didn't take it.'

'What?'

'I didn't know how big it would become. It's not my picture.'

I ask a few more questions and then I leave Armin under the wooden 'Arminland' sign hanging over the bar at the back of his house. The day has clouded over and heated up. The sugar cane is high and woolly on the way back to Brisbane.

The plot gets even thicker

It had always worried me, about the snake and the frog, that the picture might be a fake. Sure, we had checked it before. We had spoken to the person who had sent us the photo. We spoke to him twice. But how much effort do you put into disproving a harmless story that you really, really want to publish?

The editor answers: whatever it takes to sleep easy. Some stories you know the whole world is going to buy into. It's in no one's interest for these harmless, entertaining stories to be fakes. That's what makes them most likely to be fake.

I call up Ross Alford, a biology professor at James Cook University. He identifies the frog in 'the lion and lamb.jpg' immediately.

'This is a green tree frog – it has a distinctive silhouette,' he says. 'I can't be sure about the snake because I'm not an expert, but it looks like a red-bellied black snake. A red-bellied black snake would certainly eat a frog.'

Because Professor Alford is a scientist he won't commit to certainties, but he thinks the photo is authentic.

'I wouldn't be at all surprised if this was genuine,' he says. 'Green tree frogs can swim but they don't like moving water – they tend to want to get out of it.'

I make another call, to the president of the Queensland Frog Society, who asks his members and everyone agrees it is possible. No one has seen it before, but that can't be the acid test of reality.

Next step is to examine the data itself. The online service Foto Forensics analyses a compressed digital image and highlights variations in the error rate – the amount of detail the compression has removed – in different areas. A distinct difference in defined areas is evidence of one image having being dropped into another.

'The lion and the lamb.jpg' shows an almost unmarred expanse of black. It is clear. The frog was really there, on the back of the snake.

The Darling Downs, after you come down the road from Toowoomba and approach the town of Dalby, gets very flat. The grass is dry beside the road, and the paddocks stretch out. Occasionally the shades of brown are interrupted by new green wheat. All along the way you are escorted by telegraph poles with arms set at wacky 45-degree angles: it's like the engineers found the freedom to express themselves out here.

How much effort do you put into disproving a story you really want to publish? Not much, if you are in the online business. But if you happen to break the meniscus of the ocean of stories, you are in for a ride. I've done it now, and I'm starting to feel like there could be a whole book in that photograph. Back at the office they don't really get it. *I* don't get it. Three years on and I'm here following up the lead Armin gave me, taking holiday time. I have a name and I'm looking for the true source of 'the lion and the lamb.jpg'.

My rented car has an abused feel. There's a looseness in the steering and a beeping alarm sounds every time I take a corner. With a home-made map resting in my lap, I pass through the town, over the river and past the grain silos and find the turn-off. I take a dirt road until I reach an open gate with home-made signs in dripping red paint: 'NO PIGGING. PIG DOGS KILLED ON SIGHT. TRESPASSERS PROSECUTED.' I move further in. Above the ripple of tyres on the dirt road, crows and other birds are calling and there's an exotic scent on the air. The place is alive.

The name Armin gave me was 'Bernie Von Pein'. It was not hard to find Bernie. According to the internet he's 'the father of organic farming in Queensland'. He has a farm called 'Hereward'. Because Bernie comes from a time when people were comfortable having their names and addresses in telephone directories, I know where he lives and where his children live. Like Gerlach, Von Pein is not a common name.

Now I'm standing on Hereward, among a cluster of buildings: three houses, built on stumps, and a few sheds surrounded by farm equipment. Surrounding that are the fences and paddocks that make up the rest of this 850-hectare property. Like Armin's workshop, the place feels ramshackle, but here there's a lot of space between things.

Bernie is in front of me: tall, square-shouldered and ancient. Next to him are his son Doug and Doug's wife Chrissie. Bernie and Doug have white beards and enormous, strong hands. I get the impression that Doug is much shorter than Bernie, but later, looking at photographs, I will find I was mistaken. There's maybe an inch in it. It's one of those impressions your mind provides to make sense of the dynamic, and the dynamic here is clear: Bernie is the boss.

'Farming has been the only thing in my life,' says Bernie. 'I'm not a sportsman or anything. Farming has run through my parents, my grandparents – it's their experiences that have gone up into this brain.'

We are listening to a man who seems to be the essence of agriculture itself. His accent is a mix of drawn-out words and dropped endings that startles you every now and then with some unexpected sound. Bernie is Australian through and through but seems to have acquired his accent in another place entirely. Which, if the past is another country, is true.

Bernie speaks of growing up on the farm, his earliest memories of snakes and poddy calves, then of taking over and introducing a system of farming in the early 1970s that required no artificial fertilisers.

'Dad was never chemically orientated. He knew we needed a legume. Well, his life ran out, and brother and I took over the home piece here off Mum and Dad. Brothers, when they marry, quite often they don't get along too well, that's a natural thing with wives. And I had to take the place over in 1969, this home piece, or walk away. I took it over. To pay brother out, I had to borrow a heap of money. So okay, I had no money. It was a drought year, and you couldn't afford to spend money on fertiliser.'

That was the start of the organic movement in this part of the world. Bernie farmed Hereward for over 40 years, founded Biological Farmers of Australia, introduced exotic crops and dealt with drought and hardship. In all that time he never experienced a flood to rival what would hit the place at the end of 2010. By that time he had passed the stewardship of Hereward to Doug, and he was living on the coast.

*

Doug is different from his father. He seems to grow a little away from him. He talks slowly, with an air of resignation that disguises the relish with which he tells stories. Sometimes his enthusiasm gets the better of him and he ends a sentence at full volume.

Doug and Chrissie have three daughters. Their eldest, Kylie, was pregnant and due to have the baby when the flood struck and sealed Hereward off from the world. The waters crept over the banks of the Condamine, swallowed up the farm swamp and kept growing. Animals were moved into different paddocks, away from the river, as the water took over more and more of the place. Soon the benchmarks set by previous floods, even the big flood of 1956, had been passed, and they were talking about the monster of 1893. Bernie once met an old-timer who had experienced 1893, who said the farm ridges were the only thing left dry. In 2011, soon enough the ridges went under, and there were only trees and these houses on their stumps, standing in the middle of an immense lake.

'We sat watching the water rise, measuring it with sticks and things,' says Doug. 'You looked out here and all you saw was waves. I looked out the window and I thought, "If only we still had the sailboat." It was like that.'

'There were whitecaps,' says Chrissie. 'We went to bed for a couple of days with the water going gurgle gurgle, lap lap, just like you were on a boat.'

The family was anxious, moving valuables and guns to high places, but didn't panic. Suzanne, another daughter, blew up an air mattress and started floating around for fun. She had to retreat immediately because the water was alive with spiders and insects.

That's the thing about organic farms – the wildlife thrives. The whole food chain benefits from the absence of pesticides. Lots of insects, and therefore spiders. Lots of spiders and insects, lots of frogs. Lots of frogs, lots of snakes.

'At the peak, when the peak arrived, it went mirror-calm. Dead calm. That was unique.'

We get into a four-wheel drive and start bumping over the farm. Doug explains how the crop rotations and animal grazing work together. The exotic scent I smelled on arrival at the farm is fenugreek, a herb used in Indian cooking that is also a legume.

The flood peaked at night. The next day Doug and Chris got out a dinghy and rowed down here along what used to be the main drive, to check on the livestock.

'Anything dry was covered in creepy crawlies – you didn't want to put your hand on anything. There were a lot of snakes in the water. So I was letting off shots, into the water, you know, to deter the snakes from the boat. I had my handgun – I was popping off foxes as well, that had gotten stuck on fence posts.'

Doug shows me the gun. It is a spotless Smith & Wesson revolver with a long barrel, 'all properly licensed and registered'. He tells me a story of killing wild pigs with it, indicating he is pretty quick on the draw, and I believe him. All Doug's slowness disappears when he decides to move.

We are travelling along the dirt road I entered by, and Chrissie points out a small tree standing under an old gum on the fence line.

'That's the spot.'

'We saw this snake going past, and Chrissie said, "I think there's something on its back."

'It was a frog. Quite comfortable it was, and it went right by the boat. Not too far away. The snake swam up to that fence post, the frog hopped off onto the post, and then the snake backed off and went down the fence a way. It wrapped itself around the wire.'

'The thing about that snake – you would swear he was giving the frog a lift on purpose. That it went up to that fence post just to drop it off. When the frog was on the post, the snake went on its way.'

Chrissie hands me a sheet of paper. On it is the photo of the frog on the snake that Armin sent us, as well as the original, uncropped photo. Looking at this shot feels like a historic moment for me. The original is a wide-angle picture showing a shrubby tree with bright green leaves half buried in floodwater. Next to the trunk is a mostly submerged fence post and two lines of fencing wire, one barbed and one plain. There's the snake in the water, familiar, heading for the post. On its back is the frog, tiny and distinct. There is a lot of brown water in the foreground.

Chrissie is the source. Not Armin and not Doug. She is the one who, sitting behind Doug in the dinghy as the snake cruised past them with its little green passenger, struggled with the camera and got the shot just before the ride ended. The farmer's wife is the end of the line.

I ask one more question: why do they think this picture of the frog on the snake became so popular right around the world?

Chrissie answers, polite but matter-of-fact.

'It's because it's unusual, isn't it? It's just highly uncommon for a frog to ride on a snake.'

It's as simple as that.

Later, Doug brings up something that has been troubling him since he told me the story of the frog on the snake. He has been stewing on the dead foxes.

'I don't like killing things. When I go out to the paddock and see a pig or a roo, or even an introduced species, I will ask myself, do I have the right, at this present moment, to take its life? There might be an economic reason I have to remove it from the scene, but I'm not going to eradicate it, I'm not going to curse it. The curse is on me, not it.

'We cursed ourselves in the Garden of Eden. Adam and Eve were given the choice of eating from the Tree of Life and the Tree of Knowledge. They chose to eat from the Tree of Knowledge. God warned them that if they did that they would die, and begin dying from then on. [Until then] animals lived together in companionship, which is why Chrissie called [the picture] "the lion and the lamb".'

I get back in the hire car, bound for Brisbane. It's dark, and the lights of the oncoming cars are powerful. The damn alarm is still beeping in the car for no good reason and I'm sleepier than I should be. I reach over and grab something Doug gave me before I left the farm: a sprig of leaves. This is gumby gumby. Doug reckons the foliage of this rare tree can fix pretty much anything. He believes gumby gumby cured his mum's kidney cancer. I have a cold, so I bite into a leaf.

It's as bitter as anything I have ever tasted. It is like malaria medicine. I can't swallow. Saliva flows profusely. With one arm I push my bag off the passenger seat to get to a bottle of water and for the first time the beeping alarm stops. The car had been registering a passenger. False positive.

The Von Peins are good people. When the flood receded they got Kylie out and she had her baby in Toowoomba Hospital. They laugh about Armin, no trace of resentment that he took a photo off Bernie's computer when it was in his shop being repaired. It is a source of hilarity that he has a criminal record. Their religion gives them this thing that others don't have – that *I* don't have. It gives them peace and acceptance in the face of adversity. I am thinking about something Bernie said to me, fixing me with a look from beneath his shaggy brow: 'If I can put it to you … you're a witness. I can't change your heart. It's up to the Holy Spirit to change your heart, and that means you open your eyes a little bit. I can't change you.'

The big questions

I am sitting on a lecture hall stage, behind a desk with four microphones. On my right are radio comedian Mikey Robins and veteran journalist Paul Barry, on my left BuzzFeed

Australia editor Simon Crerar. In front of Simon and me are glasses of water. In front of Paul and Mikey are glasses of wine.

This is one of those things I do regularly: hold forth, with others, on the future of media in Australia. Tonight, the divisions in opinion will mirror the beverages. Simon and I are optimistic, happy to be part of organisations that are spending more each year on their newsrooms. Mikey now recognises the importance of the digital revolution, but he doesn't like recent cuts in Fairfax's newsroom staffing and he's worried. Paul, an experienced journalist and author, is familiar with the digital territory but can't shake the feeling it's all pretty shabby and cut-rate. He finds it difficult to imagine a world where a critical mass of journalists is employed online, enough to keep the bastards honest.

'The two questions are,' says Paul, 'what's the place for journalism, is it going to be possible to make a living out of it? The second is – is anyone actually going to be doing the digging, getting stuff that we can all then have an opinion about? In terms of the quality of journalism, that's where the question lies.'

They say, on panels and at conferences the world over, that journalism is in dire straits.

If by that they mean that a way of life is coming to an end, they are right. The institutionalised spending on big newsrooms is over, at least until the makers of the serious money in digital – search engines and social networks – find a use for large groups of professional writers and reporters. Even then the culture won't be the same, because those places have their roots in engineering. Instead of drinking after work, these guys will be staying back polishing up PowerPoint presentations and preparing for performance reviews.

The world of the alpha male editor, the world of subeditors and stone subs and compositors, of foul language, cheap interiors and 'the perpetually boiling urn' – all these details of the craft that produced a 'book' or a bulletin every day – they are gone. That is what people mourn so publicly. Maybe they are justified. But they dress up that emotion in language that stretches further than sadness.

When you talk about journalism as if it's something beautiful, sacred and terribly endangered, you are making a classic psychological mistake. You are thinking that 'what you see is all that there is'. You are forgetting all that could be.

I don't really know why I chased the story of the frog on the snake. I found something out, and beyond that I saw something else interesting, and on it went. Think about it for a moment: the original deceit of Armin; the words of an orphaned child at the scene of her parents' murder; the struggle over the right of the common people to sit in judgement; the kidnap of a boy; the death of a fox; the father and son. These things are fascinating. It is only the telling that is missing.

The story behind the story of the frog on the snake went beyond the elements of shareability – ticking the SENT boxes and finding a place in the NIT – and ended up as a justification for the optimism that runs through the Share Wars project.

If I stop writing now it's because, like everyone else, I have a deadline to hit. I am pretty sure journalism is going to be okay for the same reason the Von Peins believe us cursed: we always choose the Tree of Knowledge.

FROG HITCHES RIDE ON SNAKE TO FLEE FLOODS

Of all the startling images to have come out from the Queensland floods, this has to be the most unusual - a green frog hitching a ride on the back of a black snake.

Computer technician Armin Gerlach was visiting friends in the flood-hit town of Dalby, located in the state's south-east, last week when he spotted the unlikely pair.

'I felt amazement, I just couldn't believe it,' Mr Gerlach told ninemsn.

Mr Gerlach said a friend who had been affected by many floods told him animals often helped each other out during disasters.

'It's quite common when you have animals in floods or fires or disasters, they actually get together and don't do anything,' he said.

'[My friend] has seen foxes and rabbits forget their hunting instincts during natural disasters,' he said.

Mr Gerlach said he and his friends were inspecting flood damage on the property, where waters had risen to about 47cm.

By Anne Lin, ninemsn, 2011

Epilogue

Australia Square is a circle. People find that funny. One consequence of the shape of the famous building's floor plan is that you can work there for years without ever really knowing which way you are facing. It's difficult to get your bearings in a building that doesn't have corners.

The place was built in the late 1960s and is famous both because architect Harry Seidler designed it and because when it went up it was the tallest building in Australia. If that doesn't impress you, how about this: it was the tallest building in the southern hemisphere. No? Get this: the building had a revolving restaurant at the top. One minute you'd be looking at the Harbour Bridge, the next the Opera House, the next over the southeastern Sydney suburbs all the way to Botany Bay. All while you enjoyed a glass of rosé and a canapé.

The place seemed to have captured something of the naïve debauchery of the 1970s before that decade dawned. Other buildings sprouted up around Australia Square, and within nine years it had lost its 'tallest' status. By the 2000s it was like the child in the school photo who has to be put in the front row. But long after the Mateus and cocktail onions have been put away, the building retains a stately optimism that the years haven't overshadowed.

The Share Wars team worked in that building. Every morning we passed through Seidler's foyer and waited under his moulded Italian ceiling for the lift lights to bing. We were working in digital, nestled in the bosom of Sydney. The energy of the place got under our skins.

When we got to the point, in 2011, of discussing what social networks were doing to our industry, we took an optimistic view. We built an engine to collect the world's sharing data, and when in 2012 we saw what it spat out, we had the backup to go public with our opinions. Yes, news was getting messed up. But what was coming out the other end of the social network grinder was better than what went in. While everyone else was still talking about the death of journalism, we had access to different information that indicated our optimism was justified.

Look at what we discovered. The Likeable Engine was harvesting every story published on every front page of the world's most prominent news websites. Our first pass showed us that positive, awe-inspiring stories were being highly shared. People beating the odds, rising above themselves and triumphing against injustice were winning. Big breaking news stories about things that mattered were working. Even politics, if it was meaningful politics, was making the cut.

With editors being incentivised by the analytical feedback loop to prefer these kinds of stories, we could see we were heading out of the traffic-chasing days typified by Britney Spears and her spectacular meltdown.

In this world, we discovered to our surprise that dogs were more shareable than cats. That sex no longer sold and that 'report' was one of the least shareable words in the language. We had insights into story structures such as the reverse that we gained through collecting articles and storing them like items in a museum collection.

We found other highly shared stories that were not obviously worthy or high-traffic, but didn't seem to conform to old-school news values either. Take the most shared Australian story of all time: a little story about little penguins wearing little jumpers. It's cute, but is it really that cute? Only when you learn that the story was an appeal to knitters for help do you start to get it. Everyone knows someone who knits; this is a big Trigger. If enough people are exposed to the delightful image of an oily penguin dressed up like a dolly (Simple, Emotional and New/unexpected) then the story will be transmitted socially. In retrospect, it feels inevitable. But we doubt any old-school alpha-male newspaper editor ever plotted a front page based on the potency of the knitting fraternity.

We had the pleasure of discovering something new about people, just as Facebook was doing with its unprecedented experiments on a fifth of the world's population.

In that first data collection in 2012, old media brands that had made the leap to digital were heavy hitters in the social lists, happily sitting alongside the digital natives. *The New York Times*, CNN, the *Daily Mail*: these guys were dominating sharing with the kinds of stories that had defined the Share Wars project. Stories about things that happened.

Three years on, the world has changed. Our original hypothesis – that sharing would make news better – looks as naïve as the 1970s promise of sexual freedom. We're feeling slightly disorientated. We looked up from the meal on our table in the revolving restaurant and found the view transformed. Like Hegel, we thought everything was settled, and like Hegel we were wrong.

The latest 12 months of Likeable data we have analysed (March to February 2015) paints a starkly different picture from the 2012 data. Then the picture was a mishmash of colours and shapes. Now the canvas is all red and yellow. Those are the colours of BuzzFeed.

Jonah Peretti, the man whose mission has been to unlock viral content, has done so on a staggering scale. Peretti's 'experimental social content site' has 27 of the top 50 entries in the globally most shared list for the 12-month period. Another 15 are from *The Huffington Post*, the site Peretti co-founded.

The new entries are overwhelmingly *not* news stories. No event triggered the creation of 'Which classic rock band are you?' and 'What actress would play you in the movie version of your life?' These are quizzes, a form of content that at the beginning of 2014 started dominating Facebook's news feed.

The other entries in the BuzzFeed most shared list are themselves lists. 'The 100 Most Important Cat Pictures of

All Time' is a classic of the genre, created by the Beastmaster himself, Jack Shepherd. Shepherd offers the 'megalist' up with what is only slightly ironic bravado: 'Ok, this is it. This is the one. We can all finally shut down the internet and go home after this.' What follows is a remorseless and impeccably chosen series of photos that veer from humour to sentimentality and back again as human attributes are projected onto cats.

In the original batch of Likeable data we saw these 'listicles' emerging. Back then there were just three BuzzFeed stories in the top 50 shared:

- '21 worst things in the world'
- '20 pictures of tornadoes'
- '12 problems that only busty girls have'

We're not going to annoint 'the list' as successor to 'the news'. When we cut down the data sample to four months (November 2014 to February 2015) things look remarkably different again. The quiz epidemic is over, and sitting at number two in the most shared chart is BuzzFeed's mind-blowing '26 pictures that will make you re-evaluate your entire existence'. It's a list, but it's also an archetypal sharer that uses the classic driver of awe. The dialectic is rolling on.

Critics of the BuzzFeed business model point out that the organisation is horribly exposed to Facebook's feed algorithm. Seventy-five per cent of all its traffic comes from social networks and the major contributor is Facebook. The risk seems clear: if Upworthy can lose half its traffic in two months, the same can happen to BuzzFeed. A change to a single line of code in Menlo Park could jeopardise millions of dollars' worth of advertising campaigns in Manhattan. The BuzzFeed experiment would be over.

We don't think that is going to happen. Peretti himself has said that he doesn't care about Facebook algorithm changes that saw the quizzes lose ground in the top sharing lists toward the end of 2014.

'We have a big audience and we want it to grow, but we want it to be a deserved audience ... a reduction in traffic to us could be a good thing in some cases.'

Behind this 'good thing' comment is an understanding that has been guiding Peretti's amazing success. It is also the paradox at the heart of the social network news upheaval. The source of danger is the source of salvation. Peretti and his editors have a better understanding of what BuzzFeed readers want than any of the old-world legends – better than Charles A. Dana, Lord Northcliffe or Col Allan – precisely because in the platformed world the audience is fully exposed. The old boys were creating news in an information vacuum and only had to be better than the next editor. Now anyone who doesn't keep looking for the indicators of audience value loses in the long run. Incredibly, as this book went to press, Peretti recruited another weapon in his battle for global digital domination: hoax-buster Craig Silverman is the new editor of BuzzFeed Canada.

Like all new eras, the social news age has its fads and fashions, the superficial trappings that signal the world has changed. Some of these changes are crass – the long, sentimental Upworthy headlines – and some disturbing: the rise of the hoaxers. Underneath all the superficial indicators, though, is the steady transforming force of the audience. It's not happening the way 'net pioneers' hoped it would, with widespread citizen journalism and the erosion of centralised media power, but it is happening.

Our research into the nature of shareable news continues. Share Wars has partnered with the University of Sydney and ninemsn to expand the operations of the Likeable Engine. Whereas in the past the Engine collected millions of headlines and addresses, the new system is amassing the full text of articles as well. This allows a deeper level of analysis, while massively increasing the size of the database. As our University of Sydney colleague James Curran says, 'I want all the data. We'll work out what to do with it later.'

We are investigating how different types of content – slideshows and videos and quizzes, for example – affect sharing, and we are delving deeper into the linguistics of shareable words. The expanded approach has already revealed distinct sharing 'signatures' – patterns of frequency in the share counts of publishers' collective story outputs – for different media organisations and promises to help us refine our SENT and NIT schemes, making them more useful for journalists and marketers. We also expect to develop the earlier work of academic marketers like Berger and Milkman (see Chapter 4), this time from a news media point of view.

Everything we are learning points in the same direction: the key to digital success in the new world is not simply to better understand the Facebook algorithm. The key is to go where the platform providers don't want to: deeper 'inside the packet' (see Chapter 4), into the stories themselves. Here, in the narrative atoms being shuffled around networks, you find what is most valuable to people. Paradoxically, the new world of data created by the social network platform has led to insights that would hold true anywhere, whether on papyrus, in newsprint, over the telegraph or posted to a website. The story structures and topics that resonate most strongly now are the ones that will be around long after the last Facebook profile has been updated.

Recommended reading

Jonah Berger, *Contagious: Why Things Catch On*, Simon & Schuster, 2013

Chip Heath and Dan Heath, *Made to Stick: Why Some Ideas Survive and Others Die*, Random House, 2007

James Gleick, *The Information: A History, a Theory, a Flood*, Pantheon Books, 2011

Daniel Kahneman, *Thinking Fast and Slow*, Penguin, 2012

Michael Lewis, 'The king of human error', *Vanity Fair*, Conde Nast, December 2011

Jonah Sachs, *Winning the Story Wars: Why Those Who Tell (and Live) the Best Stories Will Rule the Future*, Harvard Business Review Press, 2012

Dan Zarrella, *Zarrella's Hierarchy of Contagiousness: The Science, Design, and Engineering of Contagious Ideas*, The Domino Project, 2011

Also see:

Share Wars blog, share-wars.com

Likeable Engine, likeable.share-wars.com

Hal on Twitter: @halcrawford

Andy on Twitter: @Huntzie

Hal Crawford is ninemsn's Editor-in-Chief. He began his career at the West Australian newspaper and has taught journalism at La Trobe University in Melbourne.

Andrew Hunter is Editor-in-Chief at Microsoft's MSN. He started his career as a print journalist before moving into digital media in 2000.

Domagoj Filipovic is Chief Technology Officer at cloud-based video platform provider Viocorp. Starting his career at ninemsn, he has been building software since 2004.

About Share Wars

We believe sharing will drive a new era of journalism.

Distribution methods have always shaped content production and resource allocation.

Arresting front pages traditionally sold more newspapers, so news organisations invested in crime reporters, photographers and editors.

Salacious celebrity stories boosted page views on news sites, so online newsrooms developed a more interesting but less important news mix, one that could be consumed by people in the privacy of their workstation.

Increasingly, stories are being shared among millions of readers on Facebook and Twitter. The Share Wars project seeks to understand what makes stories shareable and how this new distribution force will change work flows, roles and resourcing.

At the heart of the changes are the motivations for sharing content and how the subset of shared content relates to the total set of what is read. Sharing is a conscious action that reflects on the sharer and his or her relationship with their network. In browsing state, users often click on the first interesting link they notice. This is a private action with low investment. There is little at stake. But in sharing a link, you make a statement about yourself to your audience. The story is likely to be of consequence to you and your friends.

After analysing the sharing behaviour of ninemsn users, we've identified some elements that might contribute to a story being shared among this audience. These include deviance, humour and that element news editors have long suspected: animals. Age-old journalism drivers such as exclusivity and novelty are also important share elements.

Of course, different publications' audiences will exhibit different sharing behaviours. We recognise the work of Katherine Milkman and Jonah Berger at Wharton, who found the readers of *The New York Times* were more likely to share 'awe-inspiring' science-focused stories. We also acknowledge Yuri Lifshits at Yahoo!, whose study of 45 news sites in the USA and UK found opinion articles were the most shared.

During this project, we hope to improve our understanding of the myriad sharing forces by analysing data across the web and hopefully receiving feedback and contributions from those of you interested in the business of digital story-telling.

Our central idea is that this sharing era will irrevocably change journalism – in many ways for the better.

*

The purpose of Share Wars is to understand which types of news stories are being shared through social media and why they're being shared. The premise is that people share the stories they value.

In our experience, offering incentives for journalists to create shareable content has only improved the news mix, de-fluffed it, if anything, because people only share what they value. Fluff ruled the old days of internet journalism when the only metric journalists were encouraged to hit was page views (clicks). Kim Kardashian gets tonnes of clicks but is almost never shared.

Another concern among the audience is that journalism now is all about sharing. It's not. Important stories that are unlikely to be shared need to be produced on a daily basis by mainstream news organisations. We're suggesting tilting the focus towards sharing.

So much of what is shared is newsworthy. We don't think it's a case of selling out to social media; rather using it and understanding it and your audience to help you create and distribute great stories.

If you get a story right for social networks, it's right for everything.

Share Wars blog: share-wars.com
Likeable Engine: likeable.share-wars.com
Hal on Twitter: @halcrawford
Andy on Twitter: @Huntzie